THE TRUE STORY

of a **SHE,** a **HE,** and **HOW THEY BOTH**

GOT TOO WORKED UP about **WE**

ALTARED

CLAIRE & ELI

WATERBROOK
PRESS

ALTARED
PUBLISHED BY WATERBROOK PRESS
12265 Oracle Boulevard, Suite 200
Colorado Springs, Colorado 80921

Scripture quotations are taken from the Holy Bible, English Standard Version, copyright © 2001 by Crossway Bibles, a division of Good News Publishers. Used by permission. All rights reserved.

Italics in Scripture quotations reflect the author's added emphasis.

Details in some anecdotes and stories have been changed to protect the identities of the persons involved.

ISBN 978-0-307-73073-2
ISBN 978-0-307-73074-9 (electronic)

Copyright © 2012 by TYFTW
Illustrations © 2012 by Bruce Freeby

Cover design by Kelly Howard

Published in the United States by WaterBrook Multnomah, an imprint of the Crown Publishing Group, a division of Random House Inc., New York.

WATERBROOK and its deer colophon are registered trademarks of Random House Inc.

Library of Congress Cataloging-in-Publication Data
Claire.
    Altared : the true and ordinary story of a she, a he, and how they both got too worked up about we / by Claire and Eli.—1st ed.
        p. cm.
    Includes bibliographical references (p.   ).
    ISBN 978-0-307-73073-2—ISBN 978-0-307-73074-9 (electronic)
    1. Love—Religious aspects—Christianity. 2. Marriage--Religious aspects—Christianity.
I. Eli. II. Title.
    BV4639.C4845 2012
    261.8'3581—dc23
                                        2012013007

Printed in the United States of America
2012—First Edition

10 9 8 7 6 5 4 3 2 1

SPECIAL SALES
Most WaterBrook Multnomah books are available at special quantity discounts when purchased in bulk by corporations, organizations, and special-interest groups. Custom imprinting or excerpting can also be done to fit special needs. For information, please e-mail SpecialMarkets@WaterBrookMultnomah.com or call 1-800-603-7051.

Praise for *Altared*

"A beautifully written, searingly honest, and deeply thoughtful exploration of one of the most important topics there is."

— ERIC METAXAS, *New York Times* best-selling author of *Bonhoeffer:*
Pastor, Martyr, Prophet, Spy and *Amazing Grace: William*
Wilberforce and the Heroic Campaign to End Slavery

"Perceptive, personal, and poignantly true, *Altared* is a must-read for young Christians hungering for a realistic, biblically rich take on love and marriage in the twenty-first century."

— KATELYN BEATY, editor, *Christianity Today* and *Her.meneutics* blog

"*Altared* tells us how certain unexamined notions about courtship and marriage (often framed as 'biblical') play out among young American evangelicals today. Fresh, funny, perceptive, it is animated above all by wonder at the reality of God's love."

— JOHN WILSON, editor, *Books & Culture*

"*Altared* is a wise, wry, questioning, affirmative, sober, and deeply encouraging story—and it does something nearly unique: It asks what our thinking about 'relationships' and marriage might look like if it were governed by the biblical account of love. Not just the part about husband and wife, but love, in all its forms. This book is a sweet gift to the Church."

— DR. ALAN JACOBS, Clyde S. Kilby professor of English
at Wheaton College

"This is the relationship book for a new generation of Christians. *Altared* gently but forcefully reexamines our Christian love affair with marriage and has the audacity to suggest that real love has little to do with looking for Mr. or Ms. Right."

— DR. CHRISTINE GARDNER, associate professor, Wheaton College,
and author of *Making Chastity Sexy: The Rhetoric of Evangelical*
Abstinence Campaigns

"A much needed wake-up call—a plea for a paradigm shift in the way that we think of love, marriage, and ourselves as followers of Jesus. Eli and Claire's story needs to be shared."

—Dr. Lucy Collins, professor of philosophy, ethics, and aesthetics

"A noble and necessary book, *Altared* does the hard work of mining the Bible and Christian luminaries like Augustine, Calvin, and Bonhoeffer for insights concerning dating, marriage and love, and then delivers that truth in hearty, yet practical ways. A great gift to the reader."

—Vito Aiuto, Welcome Wagon, senior pastor of Resurrection
    Presbyterian Church

"I was challenged, entertained, taught, and inspired. The way the authors intermix biography and good, honest story telling with the more pedagogical sections is really fun and effective. Basically, it's dang good."

—Jamey Pappas, campus director, Campus Crusade, San Luis Obispo

"Now here's a strange thing: a well written, immensely thoughtful exploration of the meaning of marriage that challenges our obsession with it without devaluing it. This is a lovely and needed book that I hope everyone reads."

—Matthew Lee Anderson, author of *Earthen Vessels*

"*Altared* is a timely warning against making an idol out of marriage. In harmony (not eHarmony) with some of the best advice I ever received, this work tells readers how to pursue love, not marriage. Then see what happens. Highly recommended."

—Dr. David Naugle, chair and professor of philosophy, Dallas
    Baptist University, author of *Reordered Love, Reordered Lives*

"A real winner here. Very well and creatively written!"

—Dr. Joseph H. Hellerman, professor, Talbot School of Theology,
    author of *When the Church Was a Family: Recapturing Jesus' Vision
    for Authentic Christian Community*

CONTENTS

PREFACE

One didn't have to look far to find a marriage book in my parents' house. Neat little tomes of marital wisdom in glossy paperback could be found stacked on shelves or strewn across tables. Usually they included beaming smiles, shining eyes, straight teeth, and two fit bodies, often sweatered, clasping each other.

There were nouns like *fulfillment, intimacy,* or *satisfaction,* phrases like *finding the marriage you've dreamed of* or *the marriage you've always wanted,* written in cursive, set next to dew-dropped fruit or feet poking out of clean white sheets in sunlit rooms.

In theory, these books belonged to my parents. In practice, I read them. And they turned over in our home in roughly six- to twelve-month cycles. My family would pick a new set of relational tips and terms, flowing down from my parents' marriage, talk earnestly about them at the dinner table, put them into use for a season, and then gradually move on.

Most of the books were helpful, I think. And yet as months and years rolled by, I began to feel a certain unease with each new title. I couldn't name it, but something was missing. Not that there was something *wrong,* per se, but rather that things felt partial, like I had heard only one side of a multisided topic.

The feeling was like a drop of dye in a glass of water, fanning out in wings of color. I jostled the glass, held it up to the light, and examined it.

What was it? A hunch, not quite distinguishable, let alone something I could put a name to.

The dye spread. The more I peered at it, the more it stood out. There was *something* there, but what?

There was marriage and my adult life. There were all the tips I had read in my parents' books, all the marriage sermons I had heard from the pulpit, all my eagerness to fall in love, and all the relational quirks in my evangelical communities. In my upbringing I had learned an awful lot about marriage—both its blessings and challenges—and yet still something was lacking.

As I peered into the glass, the feeling thickened into other topics and into a range of questions about love, self-denial, obedience, loneliness, solitude, and forgiveness.

They weren't questions I asked for the sake of asking. The questions were personal. I wanted to know because I needed to know, because I *had* to know. I wanted to know for the sake of Claire and also for myself.

I can't say our story is one I'm exactly proud of, although I can't help being fond of it. The story, which is true, works something like a photo negative to the other pages here, a set of inverted colors prior to full-colored illumination.

The boy-meets-girl stuff happened long before the rest of this book came about, and perhaps could be read as our first attempt to make sense of that certain tension in our lives, the conflict between the story we'd been told since childhood and the reality in which our relationship was growing. (Our pseudonyms, by the way, help this happen.) Interwoven with the story is what came after: the exploration of the issues we grappled with. It's sort of like boy-meets-girl-and-then-they-have-questions.

Claire will tell most of the story, but I'll chime in here and there. Keep an eye on the boy/girl figures at the beginning of each chapter to clue you in as to who is talking. (And if you can help it, we recommend not skipping the analytical bits to only read the parts about two people strolling around New York. It's all mixed together for a reason.)

The goal here isn't a simplistic yes or no to marriage overall, which would be both unhelpful and a bad idea. The goal is to ask if we missed something in our evangelical assumptions about marriage. What did marriage mean for discipleship? What did discipleship mean for marriage? If Christ's love was the way others would know we are His (see John 13:35), what kind of love was it?

This book is the beginning of an answer. It is about growing up in a web of hyper-romance and sermons nudging us down the aisle. It is about how, as we get older, we rigidly define the qualities we're seeking in a "soul mate" as we look past our neighbors, our brothers and sisters, and the least of these. It is about the observation that Christians don't approach romantic relationships all that differently from the way other folks do.

It is about our growing understanding that God's plan includes more than hearts and flowers and a happy ending with rice flying in the air above a tuxedo and a white dress.

This is not a book about marriage or singleness; this is a book about love.

It began with a piece of fan mail.

An editor at a magazine I wrote for forwarded me this e-mail.

Hello!

Does anyone have contact info for Claire? I was just rereading her excellent piece and wanted to contact her about it.

Thanks,
Eli
JD Candidate
The University of Chicago Law School

October always renews a sense of novelty to New York. Summer's heat evaporates into the chilly autumn air. The spectral reds and oranges of Central Park trim Fifth Avenue with elegance. And the relief of a new start is seen in the sunburnt faces of the city dwellers. October means change.

And yet the transformation of thousands of city trees cannot compare to the turning point this brief e-mail signaled. Sitting in my fourth-floor cubicle in a publishing house in the West Village of Manhattan, I was far more delighted by the e-mail than good sense should have allowed me to be. I wasn't accustomed to fan mail, especially from someone with such an attractive e-mail signature. So with unchecked enthusiasm, I e-mailed this Eli JD Candidate back.

He responded exactly thirty-three minutes later.

Eli liked my article, but that actually wasn't his main reason for writing. He reached out to me because my byline, by then outdated, told him I was at *The New York Times,* and he wanted coverage for a website he had launched with friends. I was a little disappointed by his motives, and yet I still sensed a stroke of providence was at play.

But that was typical. I was always reading into things. Coincidences, those sneaky gleams that outline a shadow, often gave shape to my hopes. I was a catcher of coincidences, always reaching out for wisps of the un-expected and turning them over for hidden meaning. When none was revealed, I released them to the wind, only to catch another, never real-izing that all I was grabbing were the beams of light that always swirled around me, forming every moment.

Eli's e-mail was just another coincidence that I clasped to my chest. But unlike others, this beam didn't flit away when the sky moved. It steadied itself, homing in on a hope that was growing increasingly tender.

Call it love or call it silliness, but Eli's happenstance e-mail got me daydreaming. Later that night, standing under the tin ceilings of my apartment, preparing dinner, I began to color in the sketch of Eli that had formed in my mind that afternoon.

Then my roommates came home one by one. With inexplicable ex-citement, I told them all about this new website I had discovered. They were mildly interested, until they finally asked the question I was fishing for: "How did you hear about it?"

With an incriminating smirk, I told them about Eli's e-mail.

"A boy!" There were giddy screams of delight. I proceeded to gush about this dashing young man about whom I knew absolutely nothing. It wasn't long before my best friend said what I had been thinking: "Claire, I just feel something. I think he's the one!"

Their enthusiasm only fueled the fire. I tried to talk sense into my-self—and them—but failed. For the past year I had been single, and I

was tired of it. I was poised and ready for the gentleman who would cure
my plight. I had prayed desperately that God would deliver my husband
to me, and surely each day brought me closer to that, so didn't it make
sense that this e-mailer could very well be him? Yes, it was ridiculous, but
it made sense to me. I was a believer in coincidences, and Eli was perfect.
With one exception. He was in Chicago. I was in New York.

CHAPTER I

PURPLE DAYS

Alas…men talk about finding the perfect person in order
to love him. Christianity speaks about being the perfect
person who limitlessly loves the person he sees.

—Søren Kierkegaard

*Mar•riage - hap•py \'mar-ij-'hap-e\ adj 1: Having an inordinate preoc-
cupation with marital pursuits, sometimes at the cost of other Christian priorities, commonly seen in evangelicals. 2: A giddiness stemming from all
things related to marriage.*

Giddy screams of delight? Seriously?

As tempting as it is to tease Claire about her reaction to my e-mail, I
was worse. When I first e-mailed her with my website scheme, I knew
nothing about this writer from New York, but the idea intrigued me.
After only a couple e-mails, I had located her blog, was smitten with her
writing, and was certain of our future together. For some time I had been
looking for The One, and so the absence of any actual knowledge about
Claire didn't bother me much. I knew everything I needed to know,
which was that Claire was the answer to my search, my perfect match in
some cosmic plan!

Yeah, crazy, I know. I was marriage-happy, just like Claire. And in Evangelical America, where we grew up, we weren't the only ones. We were submerged in the evangelical enthusiasm for marriage, which itself was steeped in a culture that esteemed both individualism and romance.[1] Marriage was the norm, an inherent good, a biblical duty to observe. Singleness, meanwhile, was a concept batted at like a pesky fly, a vague afterthought, an exception, a gray smudge in the margin of the story God had written for each of us.

But was God as worked up about marriage as we were?

The question sounded crazy when I first asked it, but the more I thought about it, the more it troubled me. I didn't think marriage wasn't a beautiful part of life. It *is* beautiful, a good gift designed by God. But I wondered if I had made too much of it, taken a good gift and let it become too important in my heart?

As I began to sift through my influences and memories, I found marriage-happiness in a variety of forms, a sort of recurring tunnel vision with marriage at the other end. The problem wasn't marriage; the problem was how I related to it, and perhaps how Christian culture related to it more generally. Had we made too much of marriage?

Different Forms, Different Shapes

Marriage-happiness took different shapes for Claire and me, but our fervor was about the same. Claire's churches focused on purity of the heart, courtship, and gender roles, as you'll see later, whereas my churches emphasized the culture wars and sex. Two branches of the same tree, you might say. In that regard, our experiences were different, and the gap is a helpful reminder of the diversity within the church. You can't write a sentence about "the Church" and expect it to describe half the congregational experience. Denominations vary, and so do individual churches within denominations. Every faith community has its quirks.

But while the marriage quirks in my communities may not have been the same as yours, I wonder if the effect was roughly the same. Signs of marriage-y-ness could be found everywhere.

DATING ENTHUSIAST

In high school I participated in the typical hustle of congregational romance: the ups and downs of who liked whom; who broke up with whom; who got engaged (and later married, cheated upon, or divorced); and all the gossipy chatter that followed. Youth group was like the hallway of the local high school but with a bit less swearing.

In high school, the arrival of even a mildly social brown-eyed beauty was enough to cause a great frenzy. Like most teenagers, my friends and I were into love, and by that, we meant dating. Naturally, this caused headaches for our youth leaders, usually because it kept us from talking or thinking about more serious things. One leader of mine even resorted to a strict "no purple" rule on trips in an effort to institute order. The rule meant this: boys were blue, girls were pink, and due to all the chaos caused by love-induced squabbles, no mixing was allowed. Even if you were really, *really* in love, there would be no new relationships. Dating later was fine, but not on the trip. No purple was allowed, period.

As one might expect, this led to some remarkable workarounds— creative and daring—and a gentle drift toward deceit. Sermons on the difference between the "letter" and the "spirit" of the law often followed our trips, and we were always surprised by the difference.

Basically, things started out a bit marriage-happy because like most teenagers, I was relationship-happy. Finding a fifteen-year-old sweetheart was severely important, and few truths could inspire me the way she could, even though it was far from clear what I'd do once I found her.

Spouse on the Résumé

Things also seemed marriage-happy in the church because I saw few single leaders, and this is a consistent fact in all the churches I've attended.

I've heard at least a few explanations for this. One friend said she thinks churches prefer to get two ministers for the price of one. I've also heard a married pastor has experience a single pastor lacks. Some churches even *require* their pastors to have a wife. Whatever the cause, I've seen no more than two or three singles in professional or upper lay leadership in all my years in the church.

Apparently, I'm not the only one to notice this. Recently *The New York Times* profiled a qualified single pastor struggling to find a job after seminary. The reason? He didn't have a wife. In the piece, Al Mohler, the president of the Southern Baptist Theological Seminary, said, "If [young pastors] remain single, they need to understand that there's going to be a significant limitation on their ability to serve as a pastor."[2]

While I had personally never heard anything as straightforward as Mohler's view, the quote summed up a certain mood I had sensed. Serious spiritual adults in our communities were married, while single people were often seen as anomalies. The predominance of married clergy was an expression of that sentiment.

Mixed About Mixers

As I entered my late teens and early twenties, I couldn't help but see the congregational landscape ahead: college groups looked healthy and alive, while singles groups looked, uh, not so healthy. In the worst examples, singles groups were uneasy networks of adults left in some kind of limbo that always involved "mixers." It was like singles groups operated on the assumption that there was a fork in the road between marriage and single-ness, and ministry was an attempt to remedy the path not taken. Entire ministries, it seemed, were designed to get people married. No doubt some of this had to do with what singles themselves wanted, but still, where was the vision of the broader Christian life? The urgency and pur-pose toward God, one's neighbor, and the body of Christ.

I don't need to talk in the abstract to illustrate my point. Consider the website of a well-known Christian ministry. The stated goal of the website—the ministry's formal attempt to reach out to singles—was "to cast a vibrant vision for the single years," and to help prepare readers for "the challenges and responsibilities of the [season] to come."[3] Interestingly, even in "a vision of the single years," most of the tips and suggestions came back around to marriage.

Much of the content on the site is pretty obviously marriage-happy, with little balance to be found. In a particularly strong example, one of the primary editors penned a book called *Get Married*, which was writ-ten "to encourage men and empower women as you work toward your ultimate goal: a God-glorifying marriage."[4] In a similar blog post on the site, the same author provided the following advice about singleness: "To the women, I say stop glorifying the single years as a super-holy season of just you and Jesus. Yes, being single does provide you the chance to be uniquely intimate with Jesus. Enjoy that. But don't advertise it."[5]

Not all of the content on the site was quite this vivid, but most of it corresponded to my experience. On this site and in an array of singles ministries I encountered, the common goal was to rescue singles with the life preserver of marriage.

Of course, not all ministries functioned like this, nor did all Chris-tians view singles as capsized. In the best versions I saw, singles groups were healthy and functional communities, sometimes even flourishing in Christlikeness. But even when the groups functioned well, I didn't see congregations taking them seriously. Singles were looked at with pity, or curiosity, but rarely with admiration. There was always a sense of otherness.

I'm hardly the first to notice this. In his thorough book *God, Marriage, and Family,* Andreas Köstenberger writes that "post-adolescent singles are probably the most overlooked social group in the contemporary Western church."[6] When a person remains single into his or her late twenties or thirties, "many people begin to try to diagnose the problem (be it sexual orientation, physical appearance, intellectual ability, social ineptitude, unduly high standards or other factors) that has trapped the single person."[7] Undoubtedly, such attempts are offered with the best of intentions, but the underlying message is a powerful one: if a person wants to participate meaningfully in a congregation as an adult—especially as a leader—he or she probably ought to get married.

SEX-Y

Sex, of course, is another way I found traces of marriage-happiness. Obviously, for a teenage boy, sex is a *huge* deal: you guard your eyes, guard your heart, guard the heart of any girl you like, all while living as a hostage to your hormones.

Sex was an area that required guidelines and warnings, and so we talked about it a lot. And the more we talked about sex, the more we talked about marriage. Marriage was prescribed as the remedy for lust and was therefore a Really Big Deal. Marriage would be the end of all my awkward teenage sexual woes, and that created some serious expectations for marriage. I'll talk more about this in chapter 11.

Wonders for Attendance

Marriage programming was another big thing in my communities. A majority of the adults I knew were preparing to date, get engaged, marry, or rekindle the flame, and there were pastors and classes for all stages. I didn't see much marriage advice in the Bible—or at least I didn't see verses answering the questions we were asking—but that didn't slow the classes, engagement courses, and the like. Whenever a text could be nudged toward marriage, it was. At our church, there was at least one series on sex or marriage every year, and the series did wonders for attendance.

Indeed, here's a fact that suggests a sizeable demand for marriage teaching. Even Tim Keller, the pastor of Redeemer Presbyterian Church in New York City, who provides excellent warnings about the danger of an overexalted view of romance, is most popular when preaching on marriage. According to the church's website, Keller's three top-downloaded sermons of all time are, in order: "Marriage"; "Cultivating a Healthy Marriage, Part 1—Lecture"; and "Cultivating a Healthy Marriage (Parts 1 and 2)." It's not until we get to number nine that we find "Practical Grace; How the Gospel Transforms Character."[8]

The point is anecdotal, of course, but an observer may ask: Do our congregations show more demand for teachings about marriage than grace? And if we do, what does that say about us?

Textuality

As I circled back to the Bible, I didn't find nearly as much unqualified support for marriage as I might have thought. I saw some helpful metaphors and passages regarding husbands and wives, but in general, those passages floated in a sea of references about love more generally, about loving our neighbors and growing into the love that Christ called us to.[9]

In other words, Christ said little about marriage and a lot about love. *Love* appeared to be the imperative *before* marriage. Christ's teaching about love certainly applied to marriage, but it was also about so much more. And in my communities, we focused a lot on the marriage part, but less on the other stuff.

As I thought about this, it seemed like maybe my evangelical under-standing of marriage had grown larger than what could be found in the Bible. Jesus, of course, does affirm marriage in Matthew 19:5—"the two shall become one flesh"—and yet he also tells us provocatively that there will be no marriage in heaven (see Matthew 22:23–33). Jesus supports and reinforces divorce rules (see Matthew 5:31–32)—implying marriage is worthy of both fierce commitment and defense—and yet tells a story in which a man misses the great banquet because he is too busy with mar-riage (see Luke 14:12–24). Likewise, Paul charges husbands with the re-sponsibility of loving their wives as Christ loved the church (see Ephesians 5:25–33), but he also warns us that the interests of a married man or woman can be divided (see 1 Corinthians 7:33–34). A husband or wife is anxious to please not only God but his or her spouse, a "worldly thing" according to Paul, whereas the unmarried person is "anxious about the things of the Lord" (1 Corinthians 7:32–34).

Additionally, most of the main figures in the New Testament didn't marry. Jesus didn't, nor did John the Baptist and perhaps quite a few of the other disciples (at least as far as we know—although some did marry). Paul vocally advocated for singleness and was single for most of if not his entire ministry. Counting heads doesn't prove anything, of course, but here were facts I had rarely heard. Contrary to what I expected, few spouses were even mentioned at length in the New Testament, and there were few if any discussions of romantic love overall.

As I saw these pro and con marriage passages together, it seemed like the Bible was offering a slightly different perspective on marriage—or at least a more nuanced one—than what I had heard. There were beautiful marriage verses to be considered (see Genesis 2:18–24; Ephesians 5:21–33; and Hebrews 13:4, among others), and I could usually recite them by memory, but there were also verses that were somewhat less rosy (see Matthew 19:10–12; 22:23–33; Luke 14:12–24; 18:26–30; and all of 1 Corinthians 7, among others). I had no interest in overemphasizing one set of verses at the expense of the other, but I felt like I had rarely given the second set—the less-marriage-friendly verses—more than a passing glance.

TICKING OFF THE OL' CHECKLIST

Another way I saw marriage-happiness in my life was the way I understood love. And back then, when I used the word *love,* I really meant romance.

This is what "love" meant for me: I was on the lookout for a person from whom I would find fulfillment. And I thought fulfillment would arrive in terms of attraction, emotional connection, and long-term compatibility, among other criteria, including but not limited to: green eyes, a shapely face, talent, and a sparkling personality. She would need to like music, but not the wrong type; be smart, but not the wrong type of smart, and so forth. Love meant finding someone with the right attributes and ticking off the ol' checklist.

This was not the same as Christ's love. Christ's love had little to do with my checklist and seemed to focus more on the poor, the weak, and the people least likely to be wanted. Christ didn't say spouse checklists were wrong, but He did love a lot of people who wouldn't have satisfied mine.

On one side, then, I had romance; on the other, the love of Christ.

The two weren't exclusive, of course. There was no dichotomy, and I didn't have to choose one or the other. But they *were* different. And I almost always prioritized romance. I poured incredible effort into finding The One, and indeed, even my notion of Christian marriage owed more to romance as an influence than it did to Christ's example of love. I might have said otherwise in a pious moment, but if I looked at my actual life, I couldn't deny it. Before I had thought about *what it meant to love my neighbor,* I had thought extensively about *whom I would choose to love.*

To the Barricades!

Marriage-happiness also expressed itself by way of the culture wars. Focus on the Family was a significant presence on the airwaves in my town while I was growing up—I still know many plots from *Adventures in Odyssey*—and so I naturally identified the idea of Christianity with healthy families. My childhood church wasn't all that political, but we were careful observers of politics when it came to the family. Family and the institution of marriage were being broken down by society, and we were its defenders.

This isn't anything to complain about! Christians should clearly want to strengthen a structure that provides stability and critical support to so many people (and there are biblical reasons, too). But at the same time, before others knew us by our love (whether in our little town or as Christians in America), people knew us first as defenders of the family. Our reputation as defenders of the family was greater than our reputation as people who knew and practiced love.

Was this the way it was supposed to be?

The fluorescent lights were blurring my eyes. It had been an exhausting day in the office, and I still had a mound of work to finish. I stared at my computer, trying to persevere. Things were not looking good. In fact, everything was getting hazy. I turned my attention to a long-overdue e-mail from my boss and shuffled my mouse in circles. Anything but the work at hand.

Then a chat from Eli appeared.

Eli? That stranger from Chicago who had e-mailed me a few weeks ago? That's the one—except my brain registered it like this: *Eli! Brilliant! Dashing!* There was no excuse for my hyperbole, but sometimes hopes are not to be reasoned with. Within a few short weeks, Eli and I had not so subtly transitioned from random e-mails to rather in-depth online conversations. A question of mine led to a question from him. Our names glowed on each other's screens with increased frequency. Our conversations were clumsy, but *something* was afoot, and both of us knew it.

That evening, as I sat alone in the office, Eli's interruption was most welcome. Suddenly, I was stress-free and in high spirits, even grateful for my cubicle, which had provided the occasion for another conversation. We talked and teased. Banter came easily. But there was still that nagging e-mail from my boss, so I forced myself to say good-bye and get back to the grind.

An hour later, a new e-mail landed in my inbox. The subject read: "Songs for Claire to Work By." *You've got to be kidding me,* I thought. I was way too easy to woo. Turning up my speakers and clicking on the first song, I started swooning, big time.

It had only been a few weeks after the serendipitous fan mail, but a trace of amour had slipped between the lines of our dialogue. There was something—a connection—that we could feel across the bandwidth. In just a few weeks, there was new whimsy and intimacy in our interactions, and that something felt like romance. The Internet not only sustained our virtual crushes but propelled them further, resulting in more sharing of songs, more chatting at work, and an exchange of increasingly personal e-mails.

Inevitably, things continued to gain momentum after that cubicle-swooning evening. Eli sent not just songs he loved but songs he wrote. I sent him not just interesting articles but my own poems. We talked about books and discovered we were both mesmerized by the same authors. We talked about music and realized we had similar libraries. We talked about theology and Halloween costumes and the weather. Across the wavelengths, we toppled into each other, sharing our lives.

Then abruptly, everything changed.

In the middle of one of our chats one morning, Eli announced a topic change:

Eli: TOPIC CHANGE.

Me: Whoa! Give me a sec to adjust here.

Eli: So I've got nothing lined up for sure yet, but I'm considering dropping by NYC next weekend. Any chance you might be around and/or up to grab a cup of coffee?

Coffee was a sweet idea, but Eli quickly raised the ante. The next day, in an e-mail that announced he had bought his plane ticket, he asked: "Any chance I could persuade you to clear some space in the ol' calendar for dinner on Thursday night?"

Um, yes.

I had a date with Eli.

Peace muttering thoughts, and do not grudge to keep
Within the walls of your own breast:
Who cannot on his own bed sweetly sleep,
Can on another's hardly rest.

—George Herbert, "Content"

PURPLE DAYS (CONTINUED)

"Leave, Cleave, and Conceive." That was our motto. We almost put it on T-shirts.

Marriage was our trademark, our gimmick, our punch line. When you came to the college group at our church, you knew you were going to hear about husbands and wives. Marriage came up in pitches to attend events. ("You know Steve and Laura, who are now happily married, met on Fall Retreat. You should come!") It came up in our sermons. ("God loves marriage! Let's look at Genesis 2 again.") It came up between the chips and carrots at social events. ("So why not Mark? He loves God.")

The topic of marriage was unavoidable. Not only did our theology often find its way back around to it, but so did our humor, our dating, and our small group studies. Marriage was a veritable theme in our collegiate lives.

FORGONE FLIRTATIONS

My own preoccupation with marital bliss started way before college, though, and carried on even after I left the dorms. In high school, I journaled frequently about my desire for a romantic, spiritual, child-rearing partner, and I often pined for the day I coddled my own snoozing children on my shoulder.

Like many of my Christian girlfriends, I prepared myself for marriage by striving to maintain a pristine heart. Unlike Eli's experiences, in my little corner of evangelical subculture, purity was scaled back to the subtlest matters of the heart. Purity was not exclusively about sex, but rather, came so far *before* sex that flirting was often the great evil. Kissing, attention, misdirected thoughts: these were menaces to innocence. And so the whole great mass of men was sieved out through the risk they posed to our pre-married hearts. Boys weren't friends; they were Husbands or Purity Threats.

For instance, when I was a sophomore in high school, I recall going to an event at another high school where I slow danced with a guy friend—he placed his hands on my hips!—and afterward my conscience felt tattered and confused. I went home and cried out in my journal: "Have I been corrupted?"

Feelings like this were a normal part of growing up, and without question, I am grateful for the wisdom others imparted to me. I'm sure they saved me much heartache and foolishness. But a rather large side effect of framing good behavior in such a way was an out-of-proportion expectation for marriage. Because the idea behind purity was to give a whole heart to a future husband, purity led to a pretty radical expansion of marital hopes. Whatever I missed out on for purity's sake, I would find in marriage. The bliss I would share with a husband would be worth every instance of flirtation forgone. And naturally, even though it was good advice to avoid frivolous relationships, the immediate result was much higher spousal expectations.

Somehow, my desire to be a woman of God translated mainly into being a wife. I was never the girl who played dress-up with a wedding gown or had every detail of her wedding planned, and yet still the expectations were quite high. Though there were obviously exceptions, walking with Christ often felt like being slowly escorted to the altar.

The reasons for this are not totally a mystery. I read Elizabeth Prentiss's *Stepping Heavenward* and a biography of Susanna Wesley—mother of John and Charles Wesley and seventeen other children—in addition to other biographies and, of course, novels by Jane Austen, Martha Finley, and the Brontë sisters. Most of my literary appetite at the time was for stories about eighteenth- or nineteenth-century women for whom marriage was a primary preoccupation, regardless of religion or circumstances, because, well, they were eighteenth- or nineteenth-century women with few other avenues open to them. But their message didn't feel outdated to me because it was reiterated in my own life by pastors, teachers, and friends. And though in retrospect I see how grossly I misread many of these books, seeing neon lights behind every marriage reference, the fact that I interpreted everything with such a bias is telling.

Even as I moved out of high school and into college, where those old books felt dusty and distant in light of my new literary cravings—O'Connor, Morrison, Faulkner, and Robinson—I still felt fairly close to the mantra that wifehood and motherhood were a woman's highest calling. It was present in Bible studies, in sermons, in one-on-ones with my mentors. And it came from my mouth as much as from anyone else's. In essence, a vision of what it looked like to seek God had been funneled into one particular context—marriage—and I never stopped to consider that there might be any other way. Certainly I knew that following Christ required transformation on every level—not just regarding men—but those other areas seemed to be matters of secondary concern. And so as wifehood continued to dominate my vision of a Christian woman, I floundered in trying to find a holistic view of discipleship on my own.

The Marriage Dome

For me, the confusion of roughly equating marriage to discipleship burdened me with a sense of marital obligation that played itself out dramatically in my dating life. The upside was that I had little interest in dating, which seemed like a silly, possibly dangerous waste of time. The downside was when I did date, it was a cataclysmic spiritual crisis.

For example, I came very close to marrying a man I did not want to marry because I thought it was my duty. My boyfriend and I weren't ring shopping, but in our conversations, it was pretty clear that marriage was the expected outcome of our relationship. Normally, this would be fine because marriage *is* the general outcome of a serious relationship, but the trouble was that I felt sinful because I didn't have a great desire to be his wife. I thought I could bring myself around to it when I agreed to date him, but I couldn't. I was sure something was wrong with me. After all, marriage was one of God's favorite things, and it wasn't only supposed to be about warm and fuzzy feelings. Marriage was about finding someone with whom you could glorify God. So I prayed that God would give me the desire to marry my boyfriend. Rather than praying, *"Lord, is marriage what You want for me?"* Or even *"Lord, I want to obey. What are You asking of me?"* I prayed, *"God, make me love this man You have put in my life."* Not getting married wasn't even on my radar. It wasn't a matter of faith but of logic. God wanted marriage for me and had put this candidate in my life. Therefore, marrying him was inevitable. There was almost a pristine absurdity to my agonized prayer, but it all made sense in the Marriage Dome. And all that agonizing happened in the first month of the relationship, a relationship that lasted maybe, oh, three months.

MATCHING SOCKS AND BOW TIES

Was I the only marriage-happy one? When I started to ask the question not so long ago, the floodgates opened. I was shocked to learn how widespread the phenomenon was. Any time it came up, I heard single men and women bemoan in unison, regardless of what kind of church or school they attended.

Consider this story a woman in the United Kingdom sent us:

It is a truth universally acknowledged that a single woman in possession of a good Bible software program, must be in want of a
husband.

At least, that's how it seemed when I first began my
American seminary experience. Coming from a small church in
Britain, where the single men were generally over sixty and wore
matching socks and bow ties, I hadn't experienced too much of
the pressure to find myself a husband. That changed when I came
to America.

Perhaps I noticed the changed ethos when I looked out at the
Christian school's courtyard and realized that the flower beds
spelled out "I do." Maybe it was when meeting the endless stream
of teenage boys who held Greek textbooks in one hand and a wife
in the other. It could have been when a friend and I were being
rebuked for our lack of faith by daring to start a sentence with "If I
marry…" or when we overheard a young man state that, "There's
just something weird about men over thirty that are single…it's
just wrong!" It was certainly confirmed with the e-mail from leaders within my church that, as a single woman, I may want to attend an event because, "there are guys there that are really godly."

All of this was informally observed; no one officially said that
marriage was God's best for me. Yet, it was evident in the fact that
the vast majority of young people believed this to be true and
lived lives that pursued this goal, albeit often dressed up in spiritual words and sincere hearts.

Although, on reflection, sometimes they weren't dressed up
in spiritual words at all.…

"Women like you," said a Christian student to me, "you

know, Christian women close to thirty who are single, are either
that way because they had been hurt and are too scared to try relationships again and are like, bitter. Or they're always looking for
Prince Charming to sweep them off their feet and are just being
picky."

All in all, it was quite a relief to return home.

Whether from flower beds, the pulpit, youth groups, or singles'
groups, many Christians have received the impression that marriage is a
major centerpiece of the Christian life. And until one obtains that centerpiece, it is often implied, one might run the risk of not being a fully
functioning member of the community.

Lauren Winner knows what we're talking about. In *Real Sex*, she
says, "For many of my own single years, I cringed when Christians talked
about marriage. I was sick of hearing about nuptial bliss, sick of feeling
as if I wasn't participating in authentic Christian life because I wasn't
married, sick of feeling inferior to everyone who happened to be a wife."[10]

Christine Colón and Bonnie Field, authors of *Singled Out*, had similar experiences: "In the evangelical world, we kept running into the familiar refrain of 'wait,' or even worse, advice from experts telling us that
we weren't fully adults until we married, that we couldn't fully participate
in the church until we were married, that we couldn't develop fully as
Christians until we were married, or that we were sinful for not fulfilling
our God-given duties as wives and mothers."[11]

Debra Farrington, author of *One Like Jesus: Conversations on the
Single Life*, told *Christianity Today* that "Churches have unconsciously
bought into the belief that being single is being miserable. They might
pat singles' heads and say it's okay, but they don't really believe that."[12]

And listen to what Mary Jo Weaver says in her article, "Single
Blessedness."

> Single people are treated as people with a "problem" by the
> churches that are, for the most part, highly oriented to families....
> If churches do recognize single people at all, they tend to organize
> events for them in order that they can meet and marry and there-
> fore fit into the life of the church.[13]

On the other end of the spectrum there are those like Debbie Maken, author of *Getting Serious About Getting Married: Rethinking the Gift of Singleness,* who don't bemoan the plight of singles but rather are frustrated by the fact that there even are single Christians in the church. Maken is not only an advocate of marriage but she actually takes a firm stance *against* singleness. In *Getting Serious About Getting Married,* a book endorsed by figures as prominent as Albert Mohler, Maken goes so far as to say marriage is a biblical mandate and thus understanding singleness as a good thing is "unbiblical."[14] Others may not be writing books, but I wonder how many men and women unconsciously operate on Maken's thesis that there is something biblically wrong with the single life.

Now, to be clear, esteeming marriage in Christian circles is by no means a bad thing, and we should clearly cherish the gift from God that it is (see Hebrews 13:4), but when marriage is lifted far above singleness, problems quickly arise. For example, numbers. Statistics suggest that many singles have left the church or are in the process of leaving. As Barry Danylak observes in his excellent book *Redeeming Singleness,* "A recent study by George Barna suggests [unmarried adults] are significantly underrepresented in every facet of church life." Danylak analyzes the data:

> While on a typical week slightly more than half of married
> Americans attend a church service, only about one of every three
> single (adult) Americans attends. Presence at a service is much
> more likely among widowed singles than among divorced or

never-married adults. Though 23 percent of married adults additionally attend Sunday school class, only 15 percent of single adults attend. Although singles might have more discretionary leisure time for church-related activities, fewer than one in five regularly volunteer at church, attend a Sunday school class, or participate in a small group. On the other hand, singles are 50 percent more likely to volunteer their services to a nonprofit charitable group during a typical week than to offer themselves to the ministry of their church.[15]

For anyone who grew up in a marriage-happy community, this probably doesn't come as a surprise.

To make a long story short, marriage-happiness could be found on all sides. In the church, marriage was the finale of a purity race well run. It was the line across the room that curiously partitioned congregations. In the society around us, divorce rates were shockingly high, and weddings were a $70 billion industry. How was I not to be confused?

CAUSE AND EFFECT

Eli and I were sweating under the neon lights of marriage-happiness. The problem was not marriage. It was the way we viewed it and perhaps the way our communities viewed it as well. We could only see a bright, shiny marquee rather than the vast landscape around it.

It's hard to explain exactly how we got here, and one can imagine at least a few good reasons. You could say that Christians exalted marriage because we lived in a culture that exalted romance, and therefore "Christian marriage" was a way to redirect a prevailing value. Nearly everyone in our society—Christian or not—wanted a meaningful relationship. Perhaps we had tried to channel that interest into a more Christian form.

Or perhaps marriage-happiness is our attempt to rescue relationships from divorce. People were giving up on marriage sooner than ever, and many were even questioning the validity of marriage as an institution. And the damage caused by broken families is staggering.

Or maybe marriage-happiness is about sexuality, i.e., people are sleeping around a lot more, and so we nudge them to get married. Studies suggest Christians aren't all that different when it comes to sexual ethics, and so perhaps a marriage focus is applied as a remedy (e.g., "Take marriage seriously!" or "Get married before temptation overtakes you!"). Or perhaps you could make a similar point about selfishness: singles are told to get married to avoid selfishness, another huge problem in our society.

Or maybe marriage-happiness is about text. Maybe marriage-happiness isn't the result of cultural pressures but rather is rooted biblically in two passages: Genesis 1–2 and Ephesians 5. If a person takes a strong view of these verses, and many do, then perhaps these passages alone are all the explanation needed for the way things are.

In all likelihood, each rationale probably plays a part, and yet it's impossible to trace our marriage-happiness back to a single, clear explanation. Marriage-happiness has roots in each, and probably includes other explanations as well. And really, *why* marriage-happiness exists is beside the point in this book; the point is to think about what it might cost us.

A certain brother asked an old man saying, "Tell me, Father, wherefore is it that the monks travail in discipline and yet receive not such grace as the ancient Fathers had?" And the old man said to him, "Then love was so great that each man set his neighbour on high: but now hath love grown cold and the whole world is set in malice."

—*The Desert Fathers*

CHAPTER  2

LOVE THY NEIGHBOR

What is undivided love? Love which shows no special favor to those who love us in return. When we love those who love us, our brethren, our nation, our friends, yes, and even our own congregation, we are no better than the heathen.... Such love is ordinary and natural, and not distinctively Christian. We can love our [family], our fellow countrymen and our friends, whether we are Christians or not, and there is no need for Jesus to teach us that. But he takes that kind of love for granted, and in contrast asserts that we must love our enemies. Thus he shows us what *he* means by love, and the attitude we must display toward it.

—Dietrich Bonhoeffer

What is love?

The question of love—what do *we* mean when *we* say love?—is a terribly important one for anyone passing through this world. At the most significant moments in our lives, we define ourselves in terms of the love given or received. But what is it? Is it romance? commitment? a

feeling? a principle? Is it the pursuit and location of fulfillment in another? Is it all of the above at different times?

As Christians, we must wrestle with an additional, far more important question: What is *Christian* love? For those of us who follow Christ,
love ought to be anything but a formless, undefined mass. We are not left
on our own to whittle away at love according to our speculations. No, we
have been given a very specific model: Jesus. Unlike anyone else—any
religious figure or literary hero—Jesus is a true and living example of
perfect love. If we dedicate ourselves to Him, our love might still be
lumpy and cracked, troubled and incomplete, but it will be increasingly
Christlike. Our love may vary according to the pressure and heat of our
circumstances, but if we seek Him, our love should become more and
more like His.

WHAT IS *CHRISTIAN* LOVE?

After thousands of years of thought on the matter, it should be obvious
we can't compress love to fit within the bindings of a book—indeed, if we
could it would be disappointing—but we can at least consider the model
of love that Christ provided.

In its most elemental definition, Christian love is the grace-anchored
replacement of *our* notion of love with *Christ's* love, and we can begin to
explore this through two points of entry. First, the love of Christ is *a love
for God and for one's neighbor.* Second, the love of Christ is *a love for those
who do not love us in return.*

If by grace we seek to live out a love for God and our neighbor, our
natural loves will gradually move closer toward Christ's design, and the
confusion of our own affections will be replaced by the clarity of His. His
love will radically change both *whom* we choose to love, and *how* we
choose to love them.

This is no easy task, of course, and so for starters, it might help to look for the channels in our lives that sometimes direct our love away from the type of love Jesus taught us. For example, we evangelicals feel comfortable talking about how infidelity or a secular understanding of sex can impede our discipleship, but we don't often consider the challenges that could result from our own vision of marriage and family.

Before we can let our love expand into Christ's, we must unfasten our notions of love from cultural visions—secular or evangelical—and instead direct our affections to Christ, letting Him direct us from there (see Matthew 6:33). Our vision of "Christian marriage" and "Christian family"—even if offered with good intentions—must not define Christ-like love but rather Christ must be our guide. In other words, we cannot let our own notions of marriage shape our love. Love should shape our notion of marriage. And Christ should shape our love.

Of course, marriage and Christian love need not be in conflict. We do not have to choose between one or the other. But it is helpful to think about how much our understanding of love is influenced by the way we talk about marriage and how much of it is influenced by Christ. In our view, the two are not the same, though they certainly can and do overlap. And if we aren't careful, romance and marriage will frame Christ's love rather than the other way around.

CONDUITS OF CHRIST'S LOVE

We had it backward, and it wasn't until we ran headlong into our own dilemmas that we started to compare our own thoughts on love with Scripture. Sure enough, there was quite a discrepancy. We were familiar with Scripture's treatment of marriage—passages such as Genesis 2; Ephesians 5:22–33; and 1 Timothy 5:8, among others—but as for Christ's grander scheme of love, our lives revealed minimal commitment to His calling.

Jesus's commandment is this: "That you love one another as I have loved you" (John 15:12). Jesus spoke constantly about love and about obedience. And not just any love. God's love. A love that gave the earth its form, the stars their light, our hearts their beat, and our lives their meaning. Consider the inspired syllogism that Jesus relays to the disciples in John 15:9–14:

> As the Father has loved me, so have I loved you. Abide in my love.
> If you keep my commandments, you will abide in my love, just
> as I have kept my Father's commandments and abide in his love.
> These things I have spoken to you, that my joy may be in you,
> and that your joy may be full. This is my commandment, that
> you love one another as I have loved you. Greater love has no one
> than this, that someone lay down his life for his friends. You are
> my friends if you do what I command you.

The Father loves the Son. The Son loves His friends with a divine love. These friends are to love with that same love, which is at its source, the Father's. And why did He tell us this? That His joy would be in us! Love is not an ontological regiment or a woozy sensation. It is about abiding in Christ, locating His cross-shaped mold and living there. Obedience is abiding in His love.

An understanding of the Father's love ought to unsettle many of our old habits. As Christians, we are to be conduits of the Father's love. We are not just called to be seekers of marriage or sustainers of the nuclear family—though of course love may mean that for many of us. We are endowed with an even higher calling: to love one another as we have been loved.

And when Jesus says, "Love one another," He points to the most sacrificial love—a willingness to lay down even one's life. And He didn't just speak of this love, He modeled it on the cross. We are to love one another with equal abandon, and by "another," He includes even those the world forgot. Yes, we are to love our spouses and family members but also non-spouses and non-family members. Christian love does not exclude husbands, wives, and children, but it does ask for more. It is not merely about the fulfillment of our romantic hopes; it is about imitating Christ's demonstration of love to all, which culminated in His death but was also lived out daily when He ate with tax collectors, forgave prostitutes, and healed the sick.

When we focus too much on dating, marriage, and family in our communities—directing our efforts toward "successful" marriages and families, often defined in cultural terms—we risk missing out on the power of Christ's love, which transcends culture. To acknowledge this isn't to say that we shouldn't be romantic, get married, or have families, but only that we should remember that *Christ called us to imitate His love first,* and that His love might require a dramatic re-rendering of the way we approach it on our own. The free gift of grace must not leave our lives unchanged.

So first impressions are not really my thing. When I first asked Claire out to dinner in New York, the request was hardly a confident step toward togetherness. No, it was more an acceptance of inevitability: At some point, we needed to move out of the fog of daydreaming and into real life. E-mails and blurry-eyed romanticizing wouldn't be enough.

While this was exciting for me, it also presented a serious threat: I was hardly smooth when it came to introductions. As long as I could re-member, awkwardness had followed me around like a kid brother, pop-ping up at all the inopportune times. It was like I had a gift for social implosion; I could sail along smoothly in a gathering of friends, and then, without the faintest hint of breeze, capsize in full.

This awkwardness had been confirmed to me by a cross section of friends and loved ones, and I had more or less made peace with it. At best, I was told, my awkwardness meant a measure of sincerity that endeared me to others; at worst, it was a vial of social poison, ready to be spilled at the slightest jostle.

Two examples prove my case:

Specimen #1: My first serious high school crush and first kiss.

My girlfriend and I had dated for nearly a year and were a typical couple in all the typical ways. We sat through movies on the weekends and toilet papered each other's houses. Our relationship was full of the joy and effervescence of the best of the teenage years. Butterflies flapped fran-tically because they had never flapped before, and all was bright and new.

The night it happened, we stood cheek to cheek in silence for what I had thought was a reasonable amount of time. I had been building cour-age for this moment for months, and, after a great deal of debate, felt like I finally was ready to leap into the great unknown: a kiss.

I had set my resolve, reset it, and then set it again. *Okay, now!* Nothing. *Go!* Nothing. The milliseconds dragged on. My mouth was parched. I heard myself wheeze as I drew in a breath.

Then, in one moment, it happened. *Her* lips landed on *mine.* In exasperation, she had made her move.

At my moment of consequence, I had been shoved into the metaphorical bushes.

And that was my first kiss.

Specimen #2: My first serious college crush.

I was in my sophomore year of college at the time, and she was out of my league in every way. The previous summer, I had sold M&M'S packets in the snack shack at the local pool; she had lived in Milan. She was beautiful and boasted a long résumé; I was good at Nintendo and rarely cut my hair. I was bold to think she would talk to me.

I invited her to the theater in San Francisco. San Francisco was two hours away from the rural town where we lived, and I thought I would try to signal my seriousness with a sophisticated evening. She liked the arts and loved San Francisco; I liked her. The plan was airtight.

I had thought through every detail. I even took into account my '94 Honda, which was not suitable for the Most Important Night Ever. I arranged to borrow my mother's car. Given my possible selling point as a musician, I made a mix CD with a careful track list: moody, melancholy, mellow enough to talk over, but not easy listening. All was poised for triumph.

My mom gave me the thumbs-up on my shirt selection, and in a rare move, I tucked it in. I was sure I'd never looked better. Despite the fact my date lived only blocks away, I arrived early. As usual, she looked incredible, and when I opened the door of my mother's car, I could barely believe that everything had come together so well.

We sailed out of the neighborhood toward San Francisco. As we drove and drove, my eyes caught glimpses of her radiance! Then they drifted to the moonlit sky. And then back to her. And then back to the driver's wheel as I felt the sensation of lightness between my foot and the pedal below.

A lump clogged my throat. I had forgotten to gas up my mother's car! The tank was empty!

Completely empty.

Bone dry.

Now in the normal manner of things, maybe this isn't a disaster. You pull over, fill the car up, and proceed after a minor delay.

But in the rules that govern my universe, there is no small hiccup from which to recover, never only a half stumble. It's tranquility or catastrophe, and nary a note between.

We were halfway across the Bay Bridge when I felt the lightness of the pedal.

Now, for those unfamiliar with the geography, the Bay Bridge is one of three high-impact entry points into the dense metropolis of San Francisco. The five breezy lanes of Interstate 80 cram down into a thin ribbon of concrete that dangles hundreds of feet above the Pacific Ocean. Thousands and thousands of drivers cross the bridge every day, and beyond the small lanes, there is no median, no shoulder, no escape.

This, of course, is where the last drop of gas was guzzled into my own doom. I pumped the gas pedal like I had never pumped before, as if fervor would save me. It was too late. Within seconds, the car was dead, and all was done. A buzzing mass of commuters now swarmed behind my mother's car in mounting rage. Before I could even name the horror, every ounce of air had left my lungs. Even peaceful drivers began to draw out their one-fingered salutes.

This is a moment I have tried to forget. And yet, even now, two images are perfectly vivid in my memory: (1) the miles-long shockwave of traffic that pulsed backward in the rearview mirror, and (2) the sad fusion of fear and pity on my sweet date's face.

The moment was not my finest, reader, and yet it captures my gift well. The date had proceeded with ease, and then, without a moment's notice, erupted into a blazing inferno.

Have I proven my case?

Perhaps now you understand why I felt unease about this first meeting with Claire. I was thrilled to move ahead with whatever it was that we were, and yet I knew how frequently my excitement converged with almost symphonic awkwardness. What would befall us when we finally met? I had no idea.

I stared nervously into my closet. I had no idea what to wear. And to make matters worse, my best friend wasn't home. In lieu of her company I found a heartfelt note taped to my closet door in which she apologized for not being around to help me pick out my outfit on this monumental occasion in which I met, you know…him! I finally put on a black cotton dress, one that strategically could pass as "work" attire, so as to avoid looking like I had actually changed for dinner.

Throughout the day, I had been building up emotional reinforcements in preparation for finally meeting Eli. I was nervous that I wouldn't like him as much as I wanted to, so I decided to secure my affections for him before our date. Over and over again I listened to the songs he had written (such as this one: http://www.claireandeli.com/comebackhome. mp3), hoping I could make myself fall in love with him via his music. I cataloged all of our similarities in my head, so that even if he looked different than I imagined, I could fall back on compatibility. I didn't want to be disappointed. I wanted Eli to be The One.

Dress ironed, hair freshened, heels on, I sat on the couch and waited. Time moved like the opening credits in a film, slowly and expectantly. But at exactly five minutes till seven, I got a text from Eli saying he was almost there. I took a deep breath and ventured out of my apartment to meet him at the restaurant down the street.

It was a block and a half away, and so after turning the corner, I could discern a hazy figure standing outside the restaurant. Was he tall or short? Was he dressed to my tastes? Was he everything I thought he would be? The inevitable, nonvirtual meeting had arrived. I walked up to him and awkwardly introduced myself.

To my relief, Eli wasn't wearing baggy khakis or a wrinkled polo. He actually looked spiffy in his jeans and sweater. I was particularly taken with his glasses. He wasn't too tall or too short or too anything. But the situation was nevertheless almost too much to take in.

The restaurant was one of my favorites, but on this night, it felt dim and cramped. The cold I had been fighting took a turn for the worse. My eardrums thumped and my head was heavy. I remember Eli rambling on and on about Google Analytics and asking me questions about my job that I didn't have answers to. The table beside us was rowdy, and I was sure they were eavesdropping, as if I needed any more reason to be self-conscious. Eli ordered an appetizer of olives, the one item on the menu I had no interest in. Our words reverberated off the walls and never returned to us. I only managed to pick at my chicken sandwich. And there was that whole this-is-my-future-husband bit I was hung up on, and let's be honest: when you put that kind of pressure on a stranger, it's hard to not be thrown off a little when you finally meet him.

As we waited for our check, I rested my chin on my palm and studied Eli's body language. He was leaning in close, elbows on the table, head tilting this way and that. Despite the close quarters, he talked with his hands. I nodded where I thought it appropriate and tried to think of an adjective for him. *Intense?* As he had done all evening, he moved the conversation from topic to topic. *Initiating?* The check came and Eli scooped it up. *Kind?* He paid and we escaped the scene. I felt defeated.

Standing on the corner of Starr and Wyckoff, I buttoned up my coat and shoved my hands in my pockets. Eli seemed different outside surrounded by space, cooler air, and passing cars. But I wasn't in the mood for giving the evening a second chance. I needed to retreat, to escape the heaviness of my expectations. I brusquely thanked him for dinner and headed home.

LOVE THY NEIGHBOR (CONTINUED)

> With our neighbor there is life and death: for if we do good to
> our brother, we should do good to God: but if we scandalize
> our brother, we sin against Christ.
>
> —Anthony, AD 251–356

Jesus left His throne above to join our rank, reveal our reality, and tear open our world. He divested Himself of His heavenly splendor to don a carpenter's dusty shirt. And He did so with love in mind (see John 3:16). Love was the spark behind the Incarnation, and the Cross was the marker of love's essence. Christ's life sprang forth from love and His death was love's crowning achievement. It should be more than a cliché, then, when we recall what He said when given the opportunity to condense everything into one command: Love!

Love is not just one of the many laws established in Scripture; it is a command invested with marked authority: "on these two commandments depend all the Law and the Prophets" (Matthew 22:40). A love for our neighbor is elevated to just below a love for God. And so when Christ commands us to love our neighbor, it is not optional. It is a centerpiece of our identity as disciples.

Much ink has been spilled on this command because even though its words are simple, its application is certainly not. Loving one's neighbor is an unnatural love, a love that rests uneasily alongside our natural tendencies.

But sadly, the familiarity of the phrase has perhaps now obscured the clarity and impact of the demand. The maxim "Love your neighbor" is used so frequently that it has become an easy and unchallenging part of our speech, resonating only with the tips of our tongues and not the gut of our being.

Our Neighbor

To be invigorated by the great commandment, and to understand Christlike love, we must know who our neighbor is. Quite simply, all whom we cross paths with are our neighbors. To put a finer point on it, our neighbor is our spouse and family member, surely, but *also* those who are unrelated to us, those who are different in class, race, status, and interests. Our neighbor is the attractive guy but also the annoying girl. Our neighbor is the classmate on our left we've chosen to sit with and the squirmy kid to our right we haven't. Our neighbor is the homeless guy on our street corner and the mom yelling at her kid in the grocery store. Our neighbor is the driver who cuts us off and the boss who disagrees with us. Our neighbor is the person we are frustrated with right now. Our neighbor is all who are near.

Admittedly, that might sound vague, but Jesus preempted any excuse by making the command shockingly concrete with a story. In the parable of the good Samaritan (see Luke 10:29–37), a lawyer asks, "Who is my neighbor?" Jesus responds with a strange narrative about a Samaritan who finds a man, stripped and beaten, on the side of the road. This battered man is a Jew, and Jews despised Samaritans and thought they were inferior. And yet it is the Samaritan—not the pious priest or the Levite, who had also passed by—who stops and shows compassion to the man, his *enemy*. The Samaritan even carries him to a hotel and leaves him with an open tab.

The implications of this parable are nothing short of astonishing. In telling us what it means to love our neighbor, Jesus points to an act of radical, counterintuitive, unnatural charity. The priest and the Levite are well-known religious figures, and were possibly on their way to perform religious duties, but it is the Samaritan, the cultural outcast, who has compassion on the Jew. Jesus uses a Samaritan and a Jew, two people operating in utterly different spheres, to demonstrate just how miraculously the love of Christ diminishes all human distinctions.

Isn't it interesting that *this* is the story Jesus uses to define love for one's neighbor? For most of us, a spouse, parent, or sibling is our most common neighbor, and admittedly sometimes can be the most difficult to love. For each hour with a stranger, we might spend forty with a family member. And yet, rather than teach within the context of family, Jesus selects the opposite: the cultural enemy with every excuse *not* to show compassion. A classic outcast extends himself to a stranger and gives with abundance. In choosing the Samaritan to embody love, Jesus teaches us that the command to love our neighbor applies to even the loosest of all contacts: the passerby on the road.

After scandalizing our assumptions with such a tale, Jesus leaves us with only one option: "Go, and do likewise."

Loving Across

When it comes to love, we have no right to be miserly. We aren't free to decide whom we will love, even if our culture is selective. As Christians, we are called to love everyone in our path. Choosiness is not an option. In fact, if our love is growing in Christlikeness, we should find our eyes increasingly turned toward those on the margins.

Do you recall the remarkably direct instructions in the Old Testament to provide for the fatherless, the widow, the poor, and the sojourner (or immigrant)? Even when the patriarchs and their families were at the center of the biblical narrative, God wanted His people to provide for those on the fringes. If you haven't looked at some of these verses recently, they're well worth revisiting. (Exodus 22:21; Leviticus 19:10; 23:22; 24:22; Numbers 15:15; Deuteronomy 10:18–19; 14:29; 16:11–15; 24:21; 27:19; Job 31:32; Psalm 94:6; 146:9; Ezekiel 22:7; 22:9; Zechariah 7:10; and Malachi 3:5, to name only a few.)

To love our neighbor, then, is to dethrone the preferences that normally rule our love. It is to dismantle the inclinations that keep us from seeing the people we don't like. It is not to create chaos in our existing loves, or purposely harm those close to us, but to reframe them within the encompassing love of Christ. This, according to Dallas Willard, is "the ethical meaning of love in real life as taught and practiced by Jesus." He says, "You can't succeed in being ethical in act or character *unless you have abandoned having your way, fulfilling your own desires, as the rule of your life.*"[1] Loving our neighbor, then, means dethroning the partiality we use to parcel out friends, according to what they offer us. Loving our neighbor means caring for the person lying broken and naked on the side of the road. Or perhaps it means reaching out to the man who stumbles into church in tattered clothes; the kid who looks arrogant but might be lonely; the competitor who makes life difficult; the friend who has spoken behind our back. The love of Christ is a minimizer of the distinctions we might rely on to arrange our loves, and a maximizer of Christlike generosity.

The book of James says this best:

> My brothers, show no partiality as you hold the faith in our Lord
> Jesus Christ, the Lord of glory. For if a man wearing a gold ring
> and fine clothing comes into your assembly, and a poor man in
> shabby clothing also comes in, and if you pay attention to the

one who wears the fine clothing and say, "You sit here in a good place," while you say to the poor man, "You stand over there,"... have you not then made distinctions among yourselves and become judges with evil thoughts? Listen, my beloved brothers, has not God chosen those who are poor in the world to be rich in faith and heirs of the kingdom, which he has promised to those who love him? But you have dishonored the poor man.... If you really fulfill the royal law according to the Scripture, "You shall love your neighbor as yourself," you are doing well. But if you show partiality, you are committing sin and are convicted by the law as transgressors. (James 2:1–6, 8–9)

Oswald Chambers restates the sentiments in James this way: "Everyone has natural affections—some people we like and others we don't like. Yet we must never let those likes and dislikes rule our Christian life."[2] Paul says it like this: "You were called to freedom, brothers. Only do not use your freedom as an opportunity for the flesh, but through love serve one another. For the whole law is fulfilled in one word: 'You shall love your neighbor as yourself.' But if you bite and devour one another, watch out that you are not consumed by one another" (Galatians 5:13–15).

The life Jesus led makes indiscriminate love all the more clear. He dined with sinners (see Matthew 9:10; Mark 2:16); He praised prostitutes for their belief (see Matthew 21:32); He touched lepers (see Matthew 8:1–4; Luke 5:12). He called us to love our *enemies,* rather than hate them (see Matthew 5:43–44), and He told us not to seek honor when we gather with others, but to humble ourselves (see Luke 14:7–11). Jesus ignored a different organizing distinction in each example. His love reached across all social boundaries and pointed to something eternal.

This certainly doesn't mean we won't have particular loves in our lives. Jesus had a measure of particular love for Lazarus and Mary in John

11, and so did Paul for Epaphroditus in Philippians 2, as did many of the patriarchs for their kin, and David for Jonathan. But we must not forget that our Christian call is also to those beyond our preferences. To love as Jesus did is to see our neighbor as Christ does. "Because the virtues you have in mind do not shine in your neighbor," John of the Cross said, "do not think that your neighbor will not be precious in God's sight for reasons that you have not in mind."[3]

AN ILLUSTRATION

An illustration might help to make all this a bit more concrete. The other day, we saw an advertisement for the New York Police Department (NYPD) plastered on the walls of JFK Airport. The ad featured a couple of policemen proudly standing next to their police dogs with the text: "Some Dogs Only Protect Their Owners. Ours Protect Everyone."

The ad got us thinking. What if the NYPD decided one day they wouldn't protect everyone in the city but only people in Times Square, leaving everyone outside Times Square to fend for themselves? What would we say? We'd say the NYPD was out of its mind, and it wasn't fulfilling its role. The job of the NYPD isn't just to protect residents in Times Square; the NYPD is supposed to protect everyone in New York City.

The people in Times Square might not thank us for reminding the NYPD of their duty to everyone, especially if it meant less protection for them. The residents in Times Square might even feel as if they were being abandoned, and yet this wouldn't change our response. Even though protection for residents *inside* Times Square is certainly a good thing, a call for help coming from *outside* Times Square shouldn't be ignored, because the NYPD's job is to protect everyone in the city. If that wasn't so, we'd say they hardly understood what it meant to be the NYPD.

Isn't this like our lives as followers of Christ? Precisely because the NYPD is what it is, its duty is to everyone in New York. It's the law, and it's their job. Likewise, Christians are called to love not only those in our families, but anyone within our reach. A family member, spouse, or friend isn't to be treated the same as a stranger—love will require different actions in different settings, and our families and friends will naturally require much more regular attention—but a love for one's neighbor has to mean a love for others as well. We need to provide faithfully for our families (see 1 Timothy 5:8), and yet the love of Christ stretches beyond familial love to the poor, the sick, the imprisoned, the outcast. Whatever treatment we give to the least of these, we give to Him (see Matthew 25:31–46).

Of course, loving our neighbor like this goes against much of what we know. As such, it is not something that we can simply decide to do, for, almost definitely, even if the spirit is willing, the flesh will prove weak. Rather, such a command requires us first to ask for a transformation of heart, to humble ourselves before God's beautiful gift of grace. We must meditate on His words daily. We must, as abstract or familiar as it sounds, pray love into our interactions with others daily, even hourly. We need these disciplines to work Christ's open-heartedness into our lives. Only then will we stop judging people and move away from resentment and toward forgiveness.

We must pray for Christ's love to enfold ours, clasping it so completely that it begins to mold and shape us. As this happens, our interest in others will become less contingent on what they can offer us and more contingent on our participation in His love. The distinctions of the world will be shoved aside as we discover the worth implanted in each life by God's hand.

When he speaks or prays with his fellow Christians at other times, the warmth of his love reaches out to them all, friend, enemy, stranger and kin alike. If there is any partiality at all, it is more likely to be toward his enemy than toward his friend.... He does not distinguish between friend and enemy, brother and stranger. I do not mean, however, that he will cease to feel a spontaneous affection toward a few others who are especially close to him. Of course, he will and frequently, too. This is perfectly natural and legitimate for many reasons known only to love. You will remember that Christ himself had a special love for John and Mary and Peter. The point I am making is that during the work of contemplation everyone is equally dear to him since it is God alone who stirs him to love. He loves all men plainly and nakedly for God; and he loves them as he loves himself.

—Anonymous, *The Cloud of Unknowing*

Variety Café was bright, almost translucent, with its honeydew walls and whitewashed furniture. What few windows there were filled the coffee shop with morning sunlight, and the cheery baristas made up for the crowded tables. I was grateful for the mellow atmosphere because everything else that was happening that morning felt so delicate, opaque.

My roommate and I had just met up with Eli at the coffee shop. As the three of us leaned in over steaming mugs, we passed around tidbits of conversation like hot coals. I was in reset mode. The night before I had returned home from my date with Eli, collapsed on the couch, and was ready to call the whole thing off. Even a single evening of stumbling through tentative romance felt overwhelming. But when Eli texted the next morning to see if I wanted to meet up at Variety, I couldn't find an excuse to not go. My cold even felt better.

Eli worked on some schoolwork while my roommate and I read, each occasionally breaking the silence to talk. But between our bursts of conversation, a quiet unease settled in. At one point, while Eli focused on his computer screen, I lifted my eyes from my book and cautiously rested them on him. For just a moment, I could stare without interference. His face was full of decency—straight nose, whiskered jaw, a dark curl hovering over his brow. Then suddenly his eyes lifted from his laptop and met mine. I looked away, quickly, blushing. Not a minute later, I was at it again.

"Eli, have you been to New York before?" my roommate interjected. I jumped like I'd been chided.

"Actually, I've spent a couple summers here," he said.

When he talked, his bottom teeth, slightly askew, came out from under his top teeth. But he was handsome. And smart. And engaging. He was not the gentleman who ordered olives the night before. I felt like now I was meeting the Eli I had talked to over the past several weeks.

We sat there in the coffee shop for hours. With my best friend beside me, the chance of this rendezvous repeating the previous night's setback was gone. But more importantly, it was her experience of Eli that put me at ease and actually made me more curious about him. As she engaged him, I wanted to engage him. As she laughed at his jokes, I wanted to draw out more of his wit. As she relaxed, I breathed easier. It was as if I couldn't see the real Eli unless I saw him through her eyes, instead of my marriage-misty ones. It certainly took some time, but when we finally left Variety, I felt I had met a different guy from the one at the restaurant the night before. My curiosity was now trimmed with respect and admiration.

The tips of my shoes kicked at the gravel. As a natural conclusion to what hadn't always felt like a smooth-sailing weekend, Eli and I found ourselves strolling through Central Park, weaving under its leafless trees, looking more at the path than at each other.

Walking by his side, I could only half listen to what he was saying. My mind kept drifting off into an analytical fog. My feelings for Eli had been so abruptly tossed from side to side in the course of our short time together that now a drifting anxiety remained.

We continued across the park, talking or sometimes just listening to the noises around us. Then, instead of turning west out of the park, we continued north. Eli's tone changed, and I actually began to listen.

"I think it would be nice to spend more time with you, to get to know you more, but only if you are okay with that?"

A montage of the weekend replayed itself in my head. I saw that gripping and irresistible focus in his eyes as we talked over burgers. I felt again my discomfort from our first dinner. I remembered the suppressed laughs we shared during a horrible indie film. But then I recalled the nerves and dread I felt when I met him for coffee. I had enjoyed spending time with Eli, but it had by no means been an easy weekend. I felt reassured by his sincerity and how well he already seemed to understand me, but I was put off by my unmet expectations.

"I think this could be a beautiful thing," he continued.

He was right. But was it worth it? It was true that we didn't have to have everything figured out, as he continued to explain. *He* wanted more, but maybe I could do without? And as he assured me that we didn't need to make any big decisions—we could just get to know each other bit by bit—I also saw the decisions only getting bigger if we continued with things.

I was flattered by what he was saying, but what was the point in pursuing something with a guy who lived eight hundred miles away? Why venture into a halfhearted relationship that would be up against so many challenges? Unless there were fireworks that forced me into the throes of romance, I wasn't interested in trying to force a relationship to materialize. I guess I was scared of getting hurt or inflicting hurt, so in my mind a clean cut seemed best, and the sooner the better. I didn't want to drag anything out that would only be messier later on. But did I really want to say good-bye?

"I think I'm a few steps behind you," I heard myself saying.

"Love seeketh not itself to please,
Nor for itself hath any care,
But for another gives its ease,
And builds a Heaven in Hell's despair."

So sung a little Clod of Clay,
Trodden with the cattle's feet,
But a Pebble of the brook
Warbled out these metres meet:

"Love seeketh only self to please,
To bind another to its delight,
Joys in another's loss of ease
And builds a Hell in Heaven's despite."

—William Blake, "The Clod and the Pebble"

CHAPTER  3

THE TRAIN RUMBLES
THROUGH

And they devoted themselves to the apostles' teaching and
the fellowship, to the breaking of bread and the prayers.
And awe came upon every soul, and many wonders and
signs were being done through the apostles. And all who
believed were together and had all things in common. And
they were selling their possessions and belongings and dis-
tributing the proceeds to all, as any had need. And day by
day, attending the temple together and breaking bread in
their homes, they received their food with glad and generous hearts, praising God and having favor with all the people. And the Lord added to their number day by day those
who were being saved.

—Acts 2:42–47

Trains are about getting from point A to point B in a timely, efficient
manner. They rumble through town on a predetermined path, with a
sequence of stops to make and a schedule to keep. A train has a plan, and
the plan moves in one direction, with little regard for anyone or anything

beyond its path. It's no surprise that cities and towns turn their worst side to the tracks.

A park, on the other hand, is the opposite. A park has no agenda and makes no exclusions. It is welcoming, lovely, and nurturing. It is a forum for life; a congregation of unscheduled joy, laughter, and leisure. Cities bring their most important events to parks: weddings, recreation, picnics, relaxation. People bring life to the park because the park invites them in, no matter who they are. No ticket required. No schedule to obey.

The parks, in a word, are turned *outward;* the tracks are turned *inward.* The parks give unceasingly to their community; the train rumbles through.

This is a picture of how we can approach our loves: We can choose to be trains or parks. We can plan our lives with rigid precision, ignore everyone who isn't sitting beside us, and simply forge ahead with our own agenda. Or, we can be present in our lives and open ourselves up to the chaos of love.

I'm sure we can all think of examples of people in our own lives, whether married or not, who operate as trains and who operate as parks. For example, when I think of parks, I think of my friends Bruce and Julie.

On Saturday mornings, Bruce wakes up early and drives to his church to fill up an industrial-size urn of hot coffee. Meanwhile, Julie, his wife, stays home getting the kids—all four of them—ready to meet up with him and a group of friends who pitch in to provide breakfast at a park down the street. Once there, they serve the food and coffee to anyone who shows up, anyone who comes and asks. On an average Saturday, anywhere from twenty-five to forty-five homeless individuals attend.

Bruce and Julie don't have a ton of money to spare, and they certainly don't have hours of extra time, but they felt this was something God was calling them to do. They have now served breakfast on Saturdays for roughly a year, and as the crowd continues to grow, the relationships continue to deepen. Not every relationship has been easy, to be sure, and yet Bruce and Julie insist the work is worth it. More and more friends have caught wind of the work, and sometimes the number of folks volunteering almost outnumbers those coming off the streets for a hot meal.

Bruce and Julie were inspired by the similar commitment of a few friends and by God's persistent prodding in their hearts. Bruce told me he couldn't exactly describe it, but there was something different about the presence of God when he served this way.

In my view, Bruce and Julie are a great example of a park, a Christian marriage turned outward by the love of Christ. Bruce and Julie certainly could have focused on their family, and few would have faulted them for it, including me. Four kids below the age of ten is not a life for the faint of heart and can certainly demand enough love, service, and sacrifice to make one's head dizzy.

But instead, Bruce and Julie have introduced their kids to a love that hints at something deeper, a love that embodies the plain implications of the love we have been given by Christ. Bruce and Julie's call may not be for each and every family, but it was certainly God's call for them, and they obeyed it. If I asked them now, Bruce and Julie would insist they haven't done anything special, and yet they have taken time from their busy lives to provide for the least of these. And their example inspires me. It's not an either/or for Bruce and Julie—provision either for family and for their marriage, or for those in need—it's a both/and, a love that broadens marriage and family into an opportunity for something more.

LOVE IN COMMUNITY

Another example that inspired me firsthand was a community of Christians I had the chance to live with in South Asia for three months.

By the time I arrived in the South Asian city, a city of eight million, this community of Christians had already been working diligently for nearly a decade on the issue of modern slavery. For a few months, they allowed me to follow them around and witness their work.

Admittedly, I hadn't chosen to work in South Asia out of any pious concern for my neighbor, but once I arrived, I was struck by the energy of this community that was living out a radical love in both word and deed. I saw believers from around the world—Indians, Canadians, Kiwis, Brits, Americans, and Ethiopians—praying with expectation for God's work among the weakest in society. Rather than a single weekly gathering, the community met five days a week for prayer, once for each workday. They prayed together, ate meals together, worshiped together, and most amazingly, concretely worked to release captives from oppression.

I saw brilliant young mothers working long days for people they'd never met. I saw fathers acting as spiritual mentors for those without fathers in the community. I saw attorneys doing work that wouldn't offer them the prestige or money they might have found elsewhere. In any number of moments that summer, I witnessed self-denial and love, reinforced by community.

The essence of that South Asian group of believers, as I saw it then, was God and the neighbor, the distinctively Christian one. These Christians were inflamed by love and serving the men and women who were deemed expendable by society, strangers who had nothing to provide in return. The community's way of life was unintelligible apart from Christ and His call to love our neighbor.

I discovered that summer that it was one thing for a community to worship together, as I had done for much of my life, and another thing to worship with a community that was plucking the oppressed out of the hands of the violent. Worship was not an ethereal feeling triggered by song and sermon, but a state of awe directed toward a God who has called us to serve the widows and the fatherless.

THY KINGDOM COME

I should be careful not to over romanticize the South Asian community. Certainly there were challenges and failures in the group's rescue work, and certainly there was infighting at times, as there is in most human gatherings. But in my view, these challenges were largely overshadowed by the sense of urgency the group had in its work. Love was not abstract, but alive, and this kept squabbles in context.

The community was up to something powerful, something *with God,* if I can put it that way. I'm not sure I know how to describe it even now, but in this community, rescuing the oppressed wasn't a token event, an isolated act performed on a service day then celebrated the following Sunday. It was part of the fabric of their lives, and you could feel it everywhere.

There were seven rescue operations that summer that each delivered a new group of workers from a forced labor facility. The permanent staff did the work for these raids, but I was allowed to help out where I could, and they even let me tag along on a couple of the operations. To say the least, some of the things I saw on those operations made a terribly deep impression on me.

After one operation, I wrote this in my journal:

The group arrived at the village in the dead of the night. The moonlight was staggeringly bright; all was translucent and aglow in bluish green. The only audible sound was a soft rushing of the wind through the looming banyan trees. The babies of the victims were long asleep, wrapping their palms and fingertips around the bends of their mothers' necks. The little boys sulked out of the trucks, sleepy and still after a long day of waiting on the floors of the tile government hallways.

Hours before, these men, women, and children had been slaves. Now they were free, soon to be reunited with their families at home. For the last year, they had labored and suffered abuse at the hands of a brick kiln owner; now they were going home.

The Christians helped the families carry their rice sacks—which contained everything they owned: clothes, a bowl for rice, a few dusty toys—down a narrow dirt path to thatch huts, then heaped the sacks onto a small patch of grass. After the last of the belongings had been dropped in the village, nothing more than a lazy half-circle of staggered huts, all was quiet in the light of the moon. Once it became clear the Christians were leaving, several of the fathers clasped their hands together below their chins and tilted their foreheads down towards their rescuers, a sign of respect.

I had seen the body of Christ move as I have never seen it move before: the community of Christ breathing and alive, sinews, flesh and bone.

This group of families—five fathers, seven mothers, nine boys, and five little girls—had been trapped for more than a year. They had accepted a small sum of money and had been confined to work for a man who considered their lives expendable. The work was simple but hard: pulling bricks out of an oven after they had been baked. But the execution of even this small job was cruel in detail; the workers weren't allowed to wait until the bricks cooled, and so the palms and fingers of even the little boys were pockmarked with burns. Worse, the debt was structured so the loans only grew with time. The owner paid the victims such a small wage that the families had to keep borrowing to provide food for themselves, which in turn caused their debt to deepen. Unless something was done, these families would remain enslaved.

The South Asian Christians had located where these families were trapped, documented their lives in the brick kiln, then used that information to persuade government officials to raid the kiln and release the families. The community made use of patiently developed relationships to direct the benefits of law toward those who could provide no benefit in return. And so on that blazingly hot day in the middle of July, I watched this group conduct their rescue: advocates working for those without a voice, and parents and children working for those beyond familial ties. I'm not exaggerating when I say it was one of the most beautiful things I've ever seen: the sunken eyes of the victims meeting the hands and feet of Christ, Christ's body vibrant and alive, sharing all it had with those who had none.

In all this, I could find only one refrain in my heart:

Our Father, who art in heaven,
     hallowed be thy name.
Thy kingdom come, thy will be done,
     on earth as it is in heaven.

CHAPTER 4

TATTERED LEDGERS

And now you live dispersed on ribbon roads,
And no man knows or cares who is his neighbor
Unless his neighbor makes too much disturbance.

—T. S. Eliot

If we're talking about love, we should talk about Cain.

Cain is one of those characters who is at once a fully complex human but also an archetype of the most straightforward kind. Cain—the first human to come from a human—is infamous for the murder of his brother Abel. And his notoriety has traveled both into the New Testament (see Hebrews 11:4; 1 John 3:12; Jude 1:11) and into the lore of our present day. Cain deserves our attention now because of what he represents: the alternative to love.

Just as we can understand warmth better when shivering through winter, we are given an example of the absence of love to help us understand its presence. Consider this striking passage in 1 John 3:

> For this is the message that you have heard from the beginning, that we should love one another. We should not be like

Cain, who was of the evil one and murdered his brother. And
why did he murder him? Because his own deeds were evil and
his brother's righteous. Do not be surprised, brothers, that the
world hates you. We know that we have passed out of death
into life, because we love the brothers. Whoever does not
love abides in death. Everyone who hates his brother is a murderer, and you know that no murderer has eternal life abiding
in him.

By this we know love, that he laid down his life for us, and
we ought to lay down our lives for the brothers. But if anyone
has the world's goods and sees his brother in need, yet closes his
heart against him, how does God's love abide in him? Little
children, let us not love in word or talk but in deed and in
truth. (verses 11–18)

To love, John says, is to not be like Cain. Put another way, the
opposite of love is death. This is not a linguistic game of opposites.
One either loves or dies. If this doesn't add some gravitas to our love,
then perhaps nothing will. Love is not just an optional state of mind
or an occasional act. It is to consume our lives. Consider how Thomas
Merton probes the presence of love in the religious life: "[The religious life] exists not as a 'good feeling' but as a constant purpose, an
unending love that expresses itself now as patience, now as humility,
now as courage, now as self-denial, now as justice, but always in a
strong knot of faith and hope, all of these are nothing but aspects of
one constant deep desire, charity, love."[1] Love is an all-encompassing
challenge; it is a matter of abiding in God's love or abiding in death.
To not love our brother, then, is to be no improvement on Cain, the
murderer.

Love Without Expectations

Because of this, the stakes of love, we now turn to the second entry point into Christ's love: *loving those who do not love us in return.* In all the variety of ways that Jesus loved, one of the most significant traits of His love is that He loved those who did not love Him back. He loved us while we were yet sinners. He gave completely of Himself before we could give anything in return. And that is how His disciples are called to love. The idea is echoed in many places throughout the Gospels, but let's begin with the version in Luke. Christ is addressing a great multitude when He says:

> If you love those who love you, what benefit is that to you? For even sinners love those who love them. And if you do good to those who do good to you, what benefit is that to you? For even sinners do the same. And if you lend to those from whom you expect to receive, what credit is that to you? Even sinners lend to sinners, to get back the same amount. But love your enemies, and do good, and lend, expecting nothing in return, and your reward will be great, and you will be sons of the Most High, for he is kind to the ungrateful and the evil. Be merciful, even as your Father is merciful. (Luke 6:32–36)

Perhaps you've heard this passage a thousand times, but have you ever read it so carefully that you've taken it to heart? So literally that you've been inspired beyond your Cain-ness? Just like the call to love our neighbor, this passage sounds simple but is actually a deeply radical challenge: we are to love those who do not love us in return. We are to *love* our *enemies.* Not just put up with them peaceably, but love them, to will them good and pursue them with the love of Christ.

This is such a contrast to the world's love! The world's love—whether in friendships or romantic relationships—is usually founded on an assessment of who *will* love us in return. When a significant other treats us poorly enough, we end the relationship. When a friend neglects us, we resent him or her and return the neglect. When our family doesn't appreciate us, we withdraw. Unless our love has been transformed, we keep track of the love we receive or don't receive from others, filling our hearts with crumbled ledger receipts. Christ, meanwhile, calls us to more. He asks us to lend and expect nothing in return.

This notion of love is hardly isolated to Luke 6. It is repeated many times in the Gospels, in a variety of formulations. We are to forgive as we have been forgiven (see Matthew 6:12); we are to forgive our brother seventy times seven (see Matthew 18:21–22); we are to love our enemies and pray for those who persecute us (see Matthew 5:43–48; Luke 6:27–28). When someone strikes us on the right cheek, we are to offer our left (see Matthew 5:39; Luke 6:29); when a man sues us for our tunic, we are to hand over our cloak as well (see Matthew 5:40). We are encouraged to love one another as Christ loved us, by laying down our lives for our friends (see John 15:12–14). And we are told that whatever we do unto the least of these—the hungry, the stranger, the naked—we do unto Christ (see Matthew 25:31–46).

This is an unsettling call, an upheaval of how we would love if we were left to figure it out ourselves. Even more unsettling is how Christ poses the challenge to us. If we fail to love those who do not love us, He asks, how are we different from the sinners? How are we different from Cain?

MARRIAGE IN CHRIST'S LIGHT

Now let's consider this in light of the modern search for a spouse. In our culture, the spouse hunt is often largely a determination of who will love us in return, and/or who will meet a set of criteria we think will make us happy. We seek out those we enjoy; we pass over those we don't. When things sour in our relationships—which is often related to the feeling that we aren't being loved in return—we retreat. When looking for a spouse, we scrutinize traits that deliver us delight and avoid the ones that drag us down. We're looking for love with a return on investment.

This might sound harmless, or just part of the way things are, but when these habits become a primary force in our lives, they become deeply harmful and dangerous to a Christian vision of life. If selectiveness trumps love, the breadth of Christ's love gets jammed into the world's mold, stunted and cramped until it fits a romantic ideal.

When looked at this way, the search for a spouse may have less to do with Christ's love than we often think. In fact, Christ doesn't appear all that interested in teaching us how to choose a romantic Other, a person who *is* this, but *isn't* this. He says almost nothing on the topic. To the contrary, Christ repeatedly emphasizes a love that reaches all who are near. He teaches us love without a careful record of rights and wrongs, without a careful eye for return. He directs us to our neighbors, not only those in the marital running but to people who may not be able to give us companionship, intimacy, children, and security.

It might sound crazy, but what would happen if we sought to know Christ's love *before* we pursued our relational goals? What if we stepped into the full challenge of love?

LEDGERLESS LOVE

Of course, Christ's ledgerless love *should* apply to romantic relationships as well. Christian dating shouldn't just mean waiting to have sex or finding a partner through the world's process, with only one extra qualification—Is he/she a Christian?—tacked on; Christ's love should transform everything. Our relationships should be as mutually generous and selfless as Christ has been to us, the unworthy benefactors of His love.

And frankly, this is the kind of love most of us are truly looking for in the end, isn't it? It's certainly how the two of us wanted to be loved. We didn't want someone to put up with us only as long as we provided something in return, because we both knew we would fail. We didn't want love only as long as we performed well; we wanted something more, something less conditional. We wanted love that persisted through our weakness.

That said, all the conditional love that characterizes dating changes once two people get married. After a couple walks down the aisle—if they're serious about commitment—the landscape is reframed. Unlike the hopes of fulfillment that propel us forward in dating, the challenge of love presents itself in its full magnitude. The husband or wife is no longer the ethereal hope of a better life ahead; he or she is the frustrating present, the person who is at times the most difficult to love and provides the least return. Perhaps it doesn't happen right away or all at once, but marriage confronts us with our inability to love, our inability to live out the things we said in our heartfelt vows.

In that case, the love of Christ surmounts our fickleness and brings us into the challenge of loving truthfully through hardship or disappointment. If Christ is the vision, a husband doesn't condition his love on what his wife can offer, and a wife doesn't condition kindness on whether the husband lives up to her expectations. The marital commitment made until death (see Matthew 5:31–32) becomes a vehicle through which we learn to love as Christ did.

But even as we see this beautiful feature of marriage (which writers like Gary Thomas have written helpful works about), Christ's love should *still* also draw us to our neighbors outside our marriages. Marriage will sanctify us, yes, but so will love. (Recall that the verb in Ephesians 5:22–

33 is *love,* after all.) And if this is so, the Christian endeavor of marriage—the search for a spouse, marriage, and formation of families—should at each turn be accompanied by a countercultural valuation of the man on the side of the road, the stranger who needs our help, or the outcast who is ignored by the popular crowd. A Christian husband would love his wife as Christ loved us, but he would also insist on the inherent value and dignity of the stranger or enemy.

In other words, in a culture that places immense value on choice, the Christian will at all times insist on the outcast who otherwise would have never been chosen.

I'll let Claire tell you most of the story, but I need to chime in here with a correction. Reader, you should know right away that I'm more than skeptical about the claim that I was, quote, "rambling on and on about Google Analytics" on our first date. Sure, my memory may not be perfect, but this seems like a textbook case of artistic license to me—a stretching of certain facts for "dramatic effect." I beg you, reader, forgive Claire these indiscretions.

But it is true that I love olives. Who doesn't like olives?

Anyway, after the first weekend hanging out with Claire, I basically felt like I'd been hit by a pitch. After all my anxiety about the first date, I was thrilled that I hadn't struck out. I was on base! I was in play! And yet I could hardly claim success, either. I felt like I was still alive in Claire's mind based solely on the hope that I might be more compelling in the future. She hadn't given me a definite "no," and maybe I could have found comfort in this, but I had the strong sense I was about to be sent back to the minor leagues.

While we were walking through Central Park, trying to figure out what was next, I had tried to acknowledge the unease we were feeling (hers more than mine) and hoped to just keep the door open. We didn't need to make any big decision, I'd offered, and yet I'd told her I thought she was great and that we should hang out more to see where things went.

The fact is, I took a risk and came to New York City because I was so excited about the idea of Claire. The pressure of the weekend had complicated my excitement, but it hadn't squashed it. More than anything, I was just curious to know more. For that to happen, though, I needed more time with her, more conversations, more walks, more meals.

But by the end of the trip, as I boarded my plane for Chicago, I was doubtful of even one more chance to hang out. See, the day after the walk, Claire sent me a pretty heavy e-mail in which she said she didn't "have overwhelmingly strong feelings about things" and that part of her didn't even want to explore things given the distance. Naturally, I was bummed about this, and yet I could hardly fault her. We had only just met—we had hung out for three days—and we were now trying to figure out what the future might hold. The pacing of how things happened on its own was enough to smother any spark. My confidence shaken, I left New York feeling unsure.

I returned to school the following day, and friends asked how the weekend went. There was little I could say that didn't broadcast my confusion: "Uhh...good?" or "Seeing the city was fun!" Everything came out sounding muddled and doubtful.

The next day at the library as I pondered the misfire of the weekend, an e-mail from Claire popped into my inbox:

Eli,

...I really want to affirm how you approached everything. I appreciated it, and I operate well under that approach.

I needed to have it obviously stated that there is no pressure, in order to free me up to process it....

And I believe I have 1.5 more vacation days to use before the end of the year, so depending on when I can take those and how much plane tickets are costing, I may be making another trip to Chicago around December 13–14. Would you be around then?

Cheers,
Claire

TATTERED LEDGERS (CONTINUED)

The love of Christ is clearly no easy cause to take up, and it is perhaps even scandalous in relation to the cultural messages swirling around our lives. But the fact is, if we do not take the full force of Jesus's teachings to heart, we will fail. We can't expect to just stumble into living out His love.

We need to love those who do not love us in return, because, in one sense, doing so begins to bring us into greater awareness of the beauty and action of Christ. We love those who can offer us nothing because we know that we ourselves deserve nothing. We love beyond worthiness because we know that we ourselves were loved while sinners. God's grace must animate it all.

And in case we forget, the love of Christ is not just taking up the banner of the trendy cause of the moment, attending an evening of fundraising while chipping in a reasonable contribution (though love of course *will* take these forms at times). Love is caring for *your neighbor, your enemy,* and for the *least of these.* And the least of these, by definition, are the ones who have been passed over and forgotten.

It's challenging, yes, but the challenge is not an optional one, especially when Christ was so clear on how seriously He takes love: "A new commandment I give to you," He said, "that you love one another: just as I have loved you, you also are to love one another. By this all people will know that you are my disciples, if you have love for one another" (John 13:34–35).

Consider also this passage in 1 John, which is even more forceful:

Beloved, let us love one another, for love is from God, and whoever loves has been born of God and knows God. Anyone who
does not love does not know God, because God is love. In this the
love of God was made manifest among us, that God sent his only
Son into the world, so that we might live through him. In this is
love, not that we have loved God but that he loved us and sent his
Son to be the propitiation for our sins. Beloved, if God so loved
us, we also ought to love one another. No one has ever seen God;
if we love one another, God abides in us and his love is perfected
in us. (4:7–12)

If God loves us, we ought to love one another. If we do not love, we
do not know God. The absolutism of that verse is chilling: *Anyone who
does not love does not know God, because God is love.* And yet: *if we love one
another, God abides in us and His love is perfected in us.* We have been created to be vessels that pour God's love into the world, and this love is one
way people will know God. We are not called to be His judges or His
secretaries or His bodyguards. We are called to be ambassadors of His
love to one another, regardless of our worthiness. We simply need to accept His calling, and God will do the rest. He will perfect *His* love in us,
not *our* love.

As we consider this in the light of our own lives, the two of us should
be the first to admit that our habits of love lack much. And yet if one
thing is clear now, it is that the more we seek His love, the more clearly
we know the tragedy of our own love, a love that often dresses up the
pursuit of self as generosity, and a love that gets irritable and bothered
when we don't receive what we think we deserve.

But thankfully, and ever so gradually, our selfishness is being turned
outward by His love. The process is terribly unsettling, and yet there's no

doubt whatsoever that through grace His love is a stark improvement on our own. Like George Herbert said back in 1633:

> Love bade me welcome, yet my soul drew back,
>   Guilty of dust and sin
> But quick-ey'd Love, observing me grow slack
>   From my first entrance in,
> Drew nearer to me, sweetly questioning
>   If I lack'd anything.[2]

Our impatience and anger confirm that which we lack on a daily basis. But His love is drawing near, and unless we frustrate things through our resistance, His love will continue to crowd out our own. His clarity is replacing our confusion. And now that we've had even the smallest taste, our own loves are looking all the more meager by the hour.

First, my dear friends, dwell in humility and take heed that no views of outward gain get too deep hold of you, that so your eyes being single to the Lord, you may be preserved in the way of safety. Where people let loose their minds after the love of outward things and are more engaged in pursuing the profits and seeking the friendships of the world than to be inwardly acquainted with the way of true peace, such walk in a vain shadow while the true comfort of life is wanting. Their examples are often hurtful to others, and their treasures thus collected do many times prove dangerous snares to their children.

But where people are sincerely devoted to follow Christ, and dwell under the influence of his Holy Spirit, their stability and firmness, through a Divine blessing, is at times like dew on the tender plants round about them, and the weightiness of their spirits secretly works on the minds of others.

—John Woolman

A man without self-control
   is like a city broken into and left without walls.

—Proverbs 25:28

The paper was wrinkled. There was little room left to write. I had been scribbling lyrics down since lunch, and now on the subway ride home, I was crossing them out and rewriting them.

Snow falls like clichés off carolers' tongues.

Eli and I were collaborating. We were writing a song together. A Christmas song, to be exact. TBCSEP (The Best Christmas Song Ever Project), we dubbed it. And maybe it was just my excitement about trying my hand at lyrics for the first time, or maybe it was something else (probably the something else), but I was completely consumed with the endeavor.

I had no idea which syllables lent themselves to good lyrics, but I knew I wanted to impress Eli, so I wrote and rewrote, and then sent along different versions to him, acting as if I had just whipped them up at work while walking down the hall between meetings or while filling up my mug at the water cooler. The truth, however, was that I pored over them laboriously.

Out to the barn, we'll ride grandpa's old sled through cedars, your hands in my mitts. Our love will warm us like afternoon's chorus. You and me, Darling, from Christmas we'll run.

But what exactly were the rules? Was it acceptable to compose romantic lyrics together? Then again, what is a Christmas song without a little romance? Besides, there was no denying that TBCSEP was more an opportunity to flirt than to compose a creative artifact. Nonetheless, we kept it professional. And lest the song get too mushy, I made it about a Rudolph sweater.

All I want to do is hide inside your Rudolph sweater and cover my eyes with my knit cap.

Within a few short days, a really fabulous song was materializing, somewhat to my astonishment. Eli was the mastermind behind it all—I just provided the words and told him what I didn't like about some of his musical choices. But the back-and-forth between us was strangely forthright and fun. Our ability to collaborate was remarkable. And the end product, I must say, was truly memorable, even though it was all recorded on Eli's little laptop. (If you're curious, you can listen to the composition here: http://www.claireandeli.com/rudolphsweater.mp3)

Between sending musical ideas back and forth, we had fully resumed the old frequency of our Internet correspondence that had almost been extinguished just a few weeks before.

See, after Eli left New York that first weekend, something unexpected happened: I immediately wanted to see him again. It didn't make sense. All weekend I had been so wishy-washy, afraid to take it too seriously. But once he was on a plane back to Chicago, I actually missed being around him. I finally had space to breathe and the oxygen cleared the fog. It also gave me room to daydream. I regretted my initial lack of enthusiasm and feared that maybe I had scared him off for good. So, not totally sure what I was doing, I sent an e-mail offering to fly myself to Chicago for a second go.

A few e-mails finally settled with Eli's simple response:

Thanks for the kind e-mail this afternoon! It meant a lot.
A Chicago visit would be great. Those dates work well for me.
I finish my last exam at noon on Saturday the 13th, and I think
I should be hanging around Chicago until the 16th or so.

But as logistics sometimes work, Eli was the one who bought another plane ticket, not me. Just a few days after putting the final touch on "Rudolph Sweater," I was on my way to the airport to pick him up.

How difficult it is to perform the duty of seeking the good of our neighbor! Unless you leave off all thought of yourself, and in a manner cease to be yourself, you will never accomplish it.

—John Calvin

SELF-DENIAL AND THE TYRANNY OF *MINE*

There is within the human heart a tough, fibrous root of fallen life whose nature is to possess, always to possess. It covets things with a deep and fierce passion. The pronouns *my* and *mine* look innocent enough in print, but their constant and universal use is significant. They express the real nature of the old Adamic man better than a thousand volumes of theology could do. They are verbal symptoms of our deep disease. The roots of our hearts have grown down into things, and we dare not pull up one rootlet lest we die. Things have become necessary to us, a development never originally intended. God's gifts now take the place of God, and the whole course of nature is upset by the monstrous substitution.

Our Lord referred to this tyranny of things when He said to His disciples, "If any man will come after me, let him deny himself, and take up his cross, and follow me. For whosoever will save his life shall lose it: and whosoever will lose his life for my sake shall find it." (Matthew 16:24–25)

—A. W. Tozer

"God gave me a desire for a husband or wife, and therefore I know He'll provide one."

Heard this before? We have, countless times. Whether in small groups, post-breakup consolations, late-night talks with roommates, or any number of conversations with other Christians, there was often the sense that our desire for a spouse meant that God would provide one. We're not sure we ever heard it from the pulpit, but quite a few of our friends, and even ourselves at times, thought that longing for a spouse meant marriage was imminent.

But if we desire a husband or a wife, does that always mean God will provide one? We can't answer one way or the other, of course, but the breadth of the statement and the conclusions drawn from it make us uncomfortable. We ourselves often don't know the difference between our own desires and desires from God. And even if we are sure a desire is from God, can we be sure He'll fulfill it the way we think He will? It would seem that if our desires always translate into a particular outcome from God, then God becomes something like a puppet.

God clearly can and does lead us through our desires, and desires from Him can illuminate, inspire, or provide a loving reproach. At times, holy desires are just the spark we need to orient our lives away from something destructive. And yet it seems there is also wisdom in not being overly sure that God will fulfill our desires in the time and manner we expect. Any time we're positive God will give us something, we must remind ourselves that His ways are above our ways (see Isaiah 55:9), and that our desires should be humbly considered in view of who He is.

As we thought about this in light of marriage, we wondered what Christ's teachings meant for our desires in the average search for a spouse. To be sure, we need to remind no one that the desire for intimacy is a good and God-given gift, a pillar of the created order and God's beautiful design. And yet we can sometimes forget our human potential to distort that design. Sin stalks and stains the beauty of how things might otherwise be.

As we reread the Gospels, we kept stumbling upon a recurring thread of self-denial, the idea that following Christ requires us to let go of the things we have and want. Try as we might, the theme could not be dodged: everything is to be given to Him, and that includes our desires.

A. W. Tozer described the situation this way: "The roots of our hearts [grow] down into things," and this is a danger because "God's gifts now take the place of God, and the whole course of nature is upset by the... substitution."[1] Nature is upset not because the gift is bad, but because we make too much of it, because we treat it as a god rather than a gift from Him. And this is no less true for relationships, one of God's most beautiful gifts. Even marriage can risk replacing God in our hearts (see 1 Corinthians 7). So long as our hearts grow into it instead of God, the gift threatens to replace the Giver.

The more we wrestled with this, we came to see how self-denial is a helpful and particularly Christian counterpoint to this, whatever our marital status may be. If self-denial means the letting go of what we want and surrendering it to Christ, as we explore below, and if intimacy is one of our greatest cultural desires, then our desire for relationships seemed like a natural starting point for active surrender to Him. (By this we don't mean a surrender of the practice of dating or desiring someone, of course, but a surrender of its importance in our hearts to Him, of our tendency to replace first loves with seconds.) If denying ourselves is a part of following Christ, as the Gospels imply, our deepest desires should be viewed as opportunities to lay down what is dear to our hearts at the feet of Christ. The deeper the desire, the greater the risk we will give it all our allegiance.

But oddly, it seemed self-denial was rather absent from our discussions on romance and love.

LET HIM DENY HIMSELF

Jesus often describes following Him in abrasive terms: leaving your father, taking up your cross, selling all you own, losing your life, and so on. We, meanwhile, as modern evangelicals, tend to associate these losses with extreme situations, Job-like spells, or times of great martyrdom. They are not what comes to mind when we describe the typical Christian's life. The fact is, we seldom think about Christian identity in terms of living without or denying ourselves. Rather, we think about denials or deprivations as things inflicted upon us, forgetting that taking up our crosses is an act done willingly, just as Christ did. "If anyone would come after me, let him deny himself and take up his cross and follow me," he said. "For whoever would save his life will lose it, but whoever loses his life for my sake will find it" (Matthew 16:24–25).

Even as we write this, we know we've been guilty of not allowing the fullness of Jesus's words to sink into our hearts. We have looked away in order to avoid any upheaval in our lives—any disruption to our plans, schemes, and desires; we have found excuse after excuse. Perhaps intellectually both of us know that we are to deny ourselves, but in the daily practice of our lives, denying ourselves easily morphs into a convenient slogan rather than a reality.

The giving up of self is an immensely important part of Christian love. In fact, we can't even talk about Christian love without a discussion on self-denial. Frankly, we didn't realize this until we had already begun to formulate our thesis, but as soon as we picked up the thread of self-sacrifice throughout Christian history—tentatively—we were startled to find that in addition to Jesus, many of the most influential minds in our tradition described following Christ primarily in terms of self-renunciation.

Indeed, as we mulled over the writings of past Christians, our understanding of love grew vastly larger as our understanding of self-denial

grew more challenging. The more we read works about the early church—
Acts, the Desert Fathers, the lives of the saints, some of the monastic
traditions—and the more we read a range of older Christian writers—
Augustine, à Kempis, Calvin, Pascal, Teresa of Ávila, John of the Cross,
Bonhoeffer, Tozer, and Lewis—the more convinced we became that
Christian love and self-denial are often two sides of the same coin. We
cannot expect to love our neighbor as Christ did until we lay down our
lives and the preferences that rule our loves. We cannot place God wholly
first until we uproot our hearts and forsake the pronouns *my* and *mine*.

I was maybe four years old, just learning how to read, and already I had found my favorite word. Caressing one of my first books, not-so-creatively titled *My First Book of Words,* I repeated the term that captivated me: "my."

Something about *my* made my heart patter. I adored the thought. Ownership was delightful, something that not only made *me* feel special but which lent a deliciousness to the object in my possession. Those two letters carved out a space no one but me could occupy, and no one but me knew the joys of.

I put great stock in the word. I genuinely believed that any book was exclusively mine by virtue of the fact that "my" was in the title. When my older brothers wanted to look at a page, I was confused and enraged. "But it's *MY* book! Can't you see?" How could they not understand?

As I got older, my possessiveness increased. I grew particularly fond of books with a page inside that said "This book belongs to _____." Oh, the joy of signing my name on that blank!

Then a little sister came along. Suddenly, nothing belonged to me. My brothers, my parents, my toys, my room, my privacy! All had to be shared. My clinging tightened. I wrote my name on everything. I put tape across the carpet of our bedroom signifying what was mine and what was hers. I never left any ambiguity regarding what was mine. For example, the second story of our clubhouse: *my* secret office. The bottom level: *her* play area. When I couldn't claim something or when claims were disregarded, I grew fierce, jealous.

And I remained that way. I loved exclusivity. I created clubs—I must have had a new one every month—all with strict membership rules and requirements. Naturally, my sister fell short of these rules—unless, of course, she agreed to be snack person and make trips to the kitchen to fetch Doritos and Capri Suns. I had a Milo and Otis club, a Native American club, a Wiffle Ball club, a Citation Lane Gazette club, and so on. I had passwords and tests and officers. They were exclusive and they were mine.

In high school, my possessiveness became more complicated. I was desperate for a kindred spirit, that friend who would belong to no one but me. Someone to whom I would give all my confidence in return for hers. She would be mine and I would be hers. Eventually, I found just such a friend in a pen pal I met one summer. Through lavish letter writing, and even sending her a lock of my hair—a decision that seems rather creepy to me now—I wanted to claim her as mine entirely. But when I realized she had friends and family who lived in her state that were equally dear to her, I dropped her, offended by the thought.

I kept writing my name on everything. Even at eighteen, when my parents moved away from my childhood home, I took my well-worn pocketknife and carved my initials in every tree I loved. Some already had my initials carved on their trunks and branches, but still I felt the need to reinstate them. I wanted the new house owners to know that these trees would always belong to me and no one else.

As I got older, my possessiveness didn't get much better. I still clung to things. Still wanted to scribble my name on everything. Still wanted to shout "Mine!" But not surprisingly, my efforts fell short. There was something slippery about the things I clutched, an irking awareness that they weren't really mine. And I always felt slippery in the hands of others. No one could hold me. As furiously as I scrawled my name into things, something elusive remained.

I pulled into the terminal. Eli was standing on the curb, suitcase in hand and a smile on his face. The glaring airport lights made him look different, older. Suddenly, I remembered the unease of our previous weekend together. A slight vibration of panic struck my lungs. Had I been wrong to suggest we try this again?

Eli threw his suitcase in the back of my car and lowered himself into the passenger's seat. We greeted each other with extra earnestness, overcompensating for our nerves. Once the pleasantries were aside, we focused on navigating our way out of the airport. Then I hit the highway. The long, long highway.

The dark stretch of asphalt was soothing. There were few cars on the road that time of night, and with the steering wheel in my hands, I settled into a rhythm with Eli. We talked easily, and our moments of silence felt comfortable. I shuffled through my music looking for the right song. Then Eli reached into his bag and pulled out a mix he had made. "We could listen to this," he suggested. Perfect. The music gave us not only a soundtrack but a conversation piece.

It felt good to have Eli beside me. It seemed so natural for us to be driving together through Brooklyn. I was even becoming attached to his profile and stern eyes. By the time we finally arrived back at my apartment, I was excited for the weekend.

I unlocked the door to my place and gave Eli the grand tour. Though a rather meager space—three of us shared a bedroom to save on rent!—it was home. What it lacked in luxury it made up for in character. It had a tin ceiling and two long windows in the kitchen through which you could see the Empire State Building and the Chrysler Building. The white molding accentuated our picture frames and knickknacks. A hodgepodge of furniture—a secondhand couch, side tables, and bookshelves—filled the long narrow living room. It seemed like good people always found their way to our home on Willoughby Avenue. So when Eli, my roommates, and I were all sitting around the kitchen table talking, it should not have felt like anything out of the ordinary. But it did.

That was when I first really felt it: a deep connection, a sense of caring, of pride, of admiration for Eli. I loved seeing him in my kitchen, listening to him talk, and watching him become friends with my friends. I loved seeing him blush and hearing him laugh.

After my roommates went to bed, I asked him the question I'd been waiting for all night: "Do you want see the roof?"

I was living in Bushwick, Brooklyn, which isn't the most glamorous neighborhood, but the second you stepped onto our roof, it was definitely the most magical. By some stroke of luck, all the buildings between our apartment and Manhattan had maneuvered out of the way to offer us an unobstructed panorama of Manhattan's skyline.

Eli and I sat down on a blanket and stared out into the glowing city. Little time had passed between him standing on the curb at the airport and our skyline gazing, but it felt like so much had transpired. It seemed I was finally starting to feel something significant for Eli.

Sitting on the roof, my arms wrapped around my knees while Eli leaned back on his gloved hands, we talked about things that mattered, things that made us laugh. We chatted about our favorite authors, musicians, and films, as our breath evaporated into the cold. We narrated our spiritual journeys. We talked about our families. We talked about it all, the good and the bad. We found ourselves revealing more than we would have otherwise if the night air hadn't been drawing it out of us. And in the comfortable lulls of silence, I was resisting the urge to rest my head on his shoulder.

And this is the really sappy part: that night I saw my first shooting star.

[Self-denial was the term Calvin] used to summarize the entire Christian life. "Self-denial" must never be confused with self-*rejection;* nor is it to be thought of as a painful and strenuous *act,* perhaps repeated from time to time against great internal resistance. It is, rather, an overall, settled condition of life in the kingdom of God, better described as "death to self." In this and this alone lies the key to the soul's restoration....

[And yet practices of self-denial] can become exercises in more self-righteousness. How often this has happened! This dreary and deadly "self-denial," which is all too commonly associated with religion, can be avoided only if the primary fact of our inner being is a loving vision of Jesus and his kingdom.

—Dallas Willard

ELF-DENIAL AND THE TYRANNY

OF *MINE* (CONTINUED)

SELF-DENIAL AND LOVE

When you stop to think about it, it only takes a moment to realize that self-denial and love are mutually reinforcing frames that fuse together and move a Christian toward Christlikeness. A love for your neighbor without self-denial is a hollow and fleeting love. If we love only until it costs us something, our love is fickle and shallow. If we love only until we're required to sacrifice something, our love will rarely inspire. A love without self-denial is conditional love, and conditional love is the love Christ specifically called us to move beyond.

The most beautiful embodiments of love, the ones that animate our favorite movies and cultural stories, almost always include self-sacrifice. The hero dies on behalf of his nation; the lover lays down his life for the beloved. The captain remains on the sinking ship until every passenger is safe. In each instance, self-denial gives love vitality.

And if love without self-denial is empty, so too is self-denial empty without love. We may deny ourselves as much as we can for any arbitrary reason, but that won't amount to anything beautiful or good. We may give away all we have, and we may deliver up our bodies to be burned, but if we don't have love, we gain nothing (see 1 Corinthians 13:3).

In short, self-denial and love limp without each other. Self-denial without love will be a conspicuous external act and nothing more. Love without self-denial may promise great things but will call it quits when love becomes costly.

Let's break this down into a few specifics. First and foremost, to love our neighbor with Christ's love, we must often, quite simply, give up the things we want. This might mean giving financially, divesting ourselves of a purchase we've had our eye on. It might mean giving of our time or flexing our carefully guarded agendas. It might mean opening ourselves up emotionally, exchanging our own peace and comfort for the trials of another.

To love, we must give up our powerful expectations of fairness or reward. When we love the neighbor who is unlovable, and our love perseveres past the initial glow of good feelings, we may not feel much reward from the act. Indeed, loving the difficult neighbor, be it a stranger, roommate, or spouse, is often followed by the serious discomfort that flows from the loss of our preferences and from the comparisons we draw the second we feel like we've missed out on something. None of this is to say God might not repay us as He pleases, but only that Jesus didn't condition our love on a promise that we will be repaid.

But that's not all. We must also give up our preconception that we can choose whom to love, and this is most powerfully seen in the command to love our enemies. Loving our enemy, as we all know, requires an intense degree of self-denial, even more than for an unlikeable neighbor. When we truly love a neighbor, we may *sometimes* have to deny ourselves. When we love an enemy, we will *always* have to deny ourselves. Loving an enemy is incredibly difficult—and at times feels impossible. One reason it's so hard to love our enemies is that loving them might mean forgiving them. To forgive them, we must sacrifice the righteous (or unrighteous) anger we feel. Letting go of unrighteous anger isn't too bad—we all know we can be petty—but letting go of righteous anger is intensely difficult, precisely because we have defensible reasons for our anger. To truly forgive, we must deny ourselves. We must let go of our judgments. We may briefly feel like heroes for showing noble forgiveness, but when the temporary warmth of a good act fades, we either want to run from them or let the anger again sink deep into our hearts again.

SELF-DENIAL IN THE GOSPELS

Self-denial saturates Christ's teachings in the Gospels. Whether it pops up explicitly ("any one of you who does not renounce all that he has cannot be my disciple," Luke 14:33), or implicitly, as with the command to love God and your neighbor (see Luke 10:27), the theme is all over the place. So let's turn now to the Bible and look at some specific passages that make this connection between self-denial and love. Note that these examples aren't stray passages we cherry-picked for the purposes of this book. These selections sit remarkably close to the heart of Christ's teaching.

First, we have the greatest commandment. To love God with all one's heart, soul, mind, and strength necessarily requires us to make secondary all other loves. We can't fill our hearts or minds with our own loves, but we must fill them completely with God. Loving God first, and seeking first the kingdom of God, means denying the loves we might prefer to prioritize. This is what Jesus meant at the end of the book of John where He asks Simon Peter, "Do you love me more than these?" (John 21:15). It is only after Simon Peter repeats over and over again that Christ is his first and supreme love that Jesus extends His invitation: "Follow me" (verse 19).

And second to loving God is loving your neighbor (see Mark 12:31). As we've said many times now, loving the people around us rarely corresponds perfectly with the love we would prefer to show if it were up to us. As Dostoevsky memorably said through his anti-hero Ivan in *The Brothers*

Karamazov: "I could never understand how it's possible to love one's neighbors. In my opinion, it is precisely one's neighbors that one cannot possibly love. Perhaps if they weren't so nigh...."[2] To the extent we actually love our neighbor—and in a *Christian* sense, this means the neighbors we'd rather not love—we deny ourselves our natural preferences.

Third, the explicit statement in John 15 (and also in 1 John 3:16):

> This is my commandment, that you love one another as I have loved you. Greater love has no one than this, that someone lay down his life for his friends. You are my friends if you do what I command you. (John 15:12–14)

Here Jesus commands us to love one another, and how does He illustrate love? A friend laying down his life for another, the ultimate act of self-sacrifice. This is the model of love we should strive to practice; a love that denies self at the greatest cost, and the love that Christ Himself modeled for us on the cross.

The fourth place we see self-denial in the Gospels is the Lord's Prayer, where it says "your kingdom come, your will be done" (Matthew 6:10). To pray for "your will to be done" is to renounce our own will. Jesus demonstrated this for us as well. Recall what He prayed in the Garden of Gethsemane soon before His arrest: "Father, if you are willing, remove this cup from me. *Nevertheless, not my will, but yours, be done*" (Luke 22:42). Because Jesus, the Son of God, so loved the world, He renounced His own will before the Father, and it was a costly, eternally important renunciation.

Also in the Lord's Prayer, note the self-denial required in the pledge that closely follows: *"Forgive us our debts, as we also have forgiven our debtors"* (Matthew 6:12). We are called to deny ourselves the grudges that we replay over and over again in our minds.

Fifth, we see self-denial in Matthew 10:38, where Jesus says, *"Whoever does not take his cross and follow me is not worthy of me."* Taking up a cross is not a picture we typically like to imagine. The image is suffering: our Lord, bloodied and broken, walking toward His violent death on our behalf. But remarkably, this is one of the ways Jesus chose to describe what it means to follow Him. In this verse, Jesus reminds us that taking up your cross is not an extreme calling for the superholy, but a basic requirement of being worthy of Him.

There's quite a lot of self-denial in the Gospels, and we haven't listed nearly all of it. Above and beyond references of self-denial described in terms of our own will (whether for our neighbor, our enemy, or for our Father), there are also many examples of self-denial given in terms of material possessions.

Remember the rich young ruler Jesus told to sell all he had and give it to the poor (see Mark 10:17–22); or the disciples Jesus sent out to proclaim the kingdom of God, instructing them to "take nothing for your journey, no staff, nor bag, nor bread, nor money; and do not have two tunics" (Luke 9:3)? Or recall how some became disciples in the first place: Jesus either asked them to leave everything and follow Him, or they left everything on their own accord. And He again urged His followers to think differently about possessions when He told them to lay up treasures in heaven rather than on Earth where moth and rust destroy (see Matthew 6:19–21).

Jesus spent a significant amount of teaching pointing us away from material possession (a denial of accumulated goods) and also away from inflexible long-term planning (a denial of control). He instructs us not to worry about what we will eat, drink, or what we will put on, but rather to "consider the lilies of the field," who grow despite the fact they neither toil nor spin (Matthew 6:25–34). And recall that we are told to ask our Father only to "give us this day our *daily* bread" (Matthew 6:11).

And self-denial wasn't important just to the ministry of Jesus, but also to the New Testament overall. Listen to Paul, who beautifully described what it was like to follow Jesus:

> But whatever gain I had, I counted as loss for the sake of Christ.
> Indeed, I count everything as loss because of the surpassing worth
> of knowing Christ Jesus my Lord. For his sake I have suffered the
> loss of all things and count them as rubbish, in order that I may
> gain Christ and be found in him, not having a righteousness of
> my own that comes from the law, but that which comes through
> faith in Christ, the righteousness from God that depends on
> faith—that I may know him and the power of his resurrection,
> and may share his sufferings, becoming like him in his death, that
> by any means possible I may attain the resurrection from the
> dead. (Philippians 3:7–11)

Note the language of self-denial in Paul's statement: Paul has "suffered the loss of all things" and counts them "as rubbish," and Paul longs to "share his sufferings, becoming like him in his death." Paul not only thought his suffering for Christ had been worth it, but he expressed hope to *share* in Christ's suffering, that he may become like Christ in death. For Paul, all gain was counted as loss.

I threaten'd to observe the strict decree
    Of my dear God with all my power and might
    But I was told by one, it could not be;
Yet I might trust in God to be my light.

"Then will I trust," said I, "in Him alone."
    "Nay, e'en to trust in him, was also His:
    We must confess, that nothing is our own.
"Then I confess that He my succor is."

"But to have naught is ours, not to confess
    That we have naught." I stood amaz'd at this,
    Much troubled, till I heard a friend express,
That all things were more ours by being His.
    What Adam had, and forfeited for all,
    Christ keepeth now, who cannot fail or fall.

          —George Herbert, "The Holdfast"

[Think about] the stream of human lives through countless
centuries. Evil, death and dearth, sacrifice and love—what does
"I" mean in such a perspective? Reason tells me that I am
bound to seek my own good, seek to gratify my desires, win
power for myself and admiration from others. And yet I
"know"—know without knowing—that, in such a perspective,
nothing could be less important. A vision in which God *is*.

          —Dag Hammarskjöld

Just keep it casual, I told myself. *Casual!*

That should have been an easy plan, seeing as I only had Eli's voice and computer-lit sentences to go by, but I struggled to take a relaxed approach to our long-distance whatchamacallit. Though in the weeks following Eli's second visit we had agreed to just get to know each other without any romantic pressures, I kept undercutting any attempt at playing it cool with my hyperactive future-husband-assessment tests. Because I had been so conditioned to be on the lookout for a spouse, any pleasant face with facial hair triggered the husband receptor in my brain. I also had been so conditioned to hedge my affections— "guard my heart"— that any pleasant face with facial hair set off another set of defense mechanisms. The result? Obsessive hopefulness and constant second thoughts. Eli was caught between the two.

How could I not overthink things? My daydreams had been years in the making. And it seemed the longer I waited, the more my expectations grew. As they grew, so did my wariness concerning matters of the heart. I knew heartache and I knew disappointment, which made me as cautious as a cricket in a windstorm.

At the same time, how could I not let my thoughts run ahead of our agreement to take it slow? I assumed I was going to get married. Everyone told me that I would with as much confidence as if they had received a word from the Lord. I was out of college, which to many people meant I had missed out on the MRS degree—and I have to admit, I was feeling the urgency as well. And while I was thoroughly enjoying my single life in Brooklyn, I couldn't help but think how much better it would be to share it with…say…my true love. I wanted someone with whom I could make a home out of a snug apartment. If I was going to wash someone else's dishes, I wanted them to be my husband's. If I was going to have a picnic in a park, how much lovelier if I could lean against him as I poured the hot chocolate. At times, even before I met Eli, my desire for that future Someone was so strong I couldn't contain it, so I wrote little letters to my future husband. They are super embarrassing and so indicative of the marriage-y-ness that was in my heart. But while it's more than a little mortifying to share them with the world, here they are for your snickers, straight from my journal.

—

Darling Sir, today I went to church without you again. I wished you were there. I wanted to link arms with you during the sermon and hold your hand during prayer, lean up against your knit sweater during brunch and pat your knee as we waited for everyone to figure out the check. Maybe next time.

—

Darling Sir, I sometimes think it is better I have not met you yet because I have time to be selfish and write. I think about how when I do meet you, you will know to sometimes let me be selfish with my time and zone out in order to write. But then, I think there is not as much pleasure in writing without knowing you because I want you to be able to read and appreciate what I write. Your opinion matters the most.

—

Darling Sir, I keep thinking that maybe you are this person I'm about to meet, or you are that man who loved my article, or you are the new person who is joining my small group. It is rather distracting.

———

Darling Sir! Where in the world are you?! I am alone in my apartment and I hear a mouse and I'm scared. I had no idea I was even a little frightened of mice. Our tiny roaches didn't bother me, but this! I can't handle it alone. I need you here so you can just take care of all of it for me while I close my eyes and let it pass. And for a second, I even wish I wasn't in New York City but in a small country home with you curled up by the fire. Mice in the country seem so much friendlier.

———

Darling Sir, sometimes it is so hard to be lonely. I'm not always lonely, and sometimes when I am I rather enjoy it, but right now, sitting alone on a quiet evening in my black leggings and with so many frustrations within me, I just want some strong safe arms around me, and I want someone that I can talk to without any kind of filter. I just need someone like that right now. The fact that you are not here to be that person I need so badly makes me, well, it just makes me sad. Very sad. So I just hope you come soon 'cause I'm ever so lonely.

———

Knit sweaters at brunch? Squealing for help because of a mouse? *Oy vey!* I had clearly been soaking in the romantic waters for far too long. A few too many chick flicks and too much time to myself had put reality out of arm's reach.

I had it bad! This, my friends, was what Eli had walked into. That line about "the man who loved my article"? Yep, that was him. He was entering a minefield. And though I had every intention of getting to know Eli without any undue pressure, I didn't always succeed because the grooves of my affections had long ago been etched by years of well-kept desires.

So what did I do? I panicked. Quite frequently. See, relationships tend to do two things to me: excite and confuse. And for whatever reason, the confusion always seems more real. Eli was no exception. I was excited by the possibility of us, but I could only see him against the backdrop of a list of things I needed—or wanted. It was like trying to look at the constellations through a pinhole planetarium. I knew better, but my feelings, or even the slightest reciprocation, were still more or less conditional on how Eli scored against my "list," which was really more like an elaborate matrix of performance metrics. Not surprisingly, this left me confused. Conditional love is baffling since sometimes it's there, but in an instant it can be gone.

Now just to clarify, my own marriage-happiness was a problem not because it isn't wise to think of a boyfriend in light of husband-potential, but for other reasons. In fact, I think it probably isn't such a good idea to date someone without any thought of whether that person might be a future spouse. So for me, the problem was (a) blindly assuming there was a future husband for me, (b) operating off that assumption immediately with Eli, and (c) asking God only about *whom* I should marry, not *what* He wanted me to do. Because Eli was a guy and I was a girl, the second he entered my life, I could only think of my interactions with him in light of marriage. As a result, I put a serious amount of unnecessary pressure on all of our interactions. Even worse, I didn't allow myself to see Eli as a brother in Christ, as a neighbor who could be part of my Christian family and with whom our "hearts may be encouraged, being knit together in love, to reach all the riches of full assurance of understanding and the knowledge of God's mystery, which is Christ," as it says in Colossians 2:2. My marriage assumptions skewed my interactions with Eli, often causing me to use him or to calculate what he could do for me. And if he could do zilch, meaning he couldn't be my husband, he was of little use. That, obviously, was a problem.

With Eli, things were beginning to feel more solid and real, but even more confusing because as my feelings for him grew, so did my expectations. As I saw something new I liked, I was also made aware of something I didn't like. Rationally, I knew I was being ridiculous, but I couldn't communicate that to my heart. Love, for me, was a set of met expectations.

CHAPTER 6

THOSE WHO HAVE FLUNG THEMSELVES

I have found the paradox, that if you love until it hurts, there can be no more hurt, only more love.

—Mother Teresa

There is no shortage of good days. It is good lives that are hard to come by. A life of good days lived in the senses is not enough. The life of sensation is the life of greed; it requires more and more. The life of the spirit requires less and less; time is ample and passage sweet.

—Annie Dillard

Stories of self-denial are abundant in the Christian tradition. But if you are like us, you might have forgotten—or never even heard of—some of the incredible men and women of faith who offered a dramatic rendering of Christ's vision for discipleship. Even though the theme of denying oneself for Christ is significant throughout Christian history, today we seem to have forgotten about the beauty of self-denial. Indeed, we (ourselves included) often drift into thinking of Christianity as a Christ-colored version of our existing lives rather than as a complete upheaval.

There's a lot we can learn from a few significant figures in our Christian lineage, and we personally have grown much from reading their reflections. We'll look at just a few of these figures, knowing there are more than we could ever discuss here.

WILLIAM JAMES

We'll start with William James, the influential Harvard psychologist and philosopher, best known for his 1901 lecture-series-turned-book, *The Varieties of Religious Experience.*

James's lecture series is not in itself a Christian work (and therefore not technically part of the "Christian tradition"), and yet it provides a fascinating overview of recorded religious experience from people as diverse as George Fox and Jonathan Edwards to Leo Tolstoy and Ralph Waldo Emerson. A strong majority of the experiences in the book would be considered traditionally Christian, though a few are not.

The purpose of James's study was an interesting one: By looking at religious experience from the perspective of an academic, James wanted to convince his friends and correspondents (a group that included thinkers as diverse as Oliver Wendell Holmes, Bertrand Russell, John Dewey, Mark Twain, and Sigmund Freud) that religious experience was valuable and worth study in the university setting.

Among other things, James identified and described several "traits of saintliness" that he found widely present through the history of religious experience. In the vast trail of testimonies and biographies James read as he assembled his lectures, one of the five traits he found most consistently was self-denial. Here's how James put it:

Throughout the annals of the saintly life, we find this ever-recur-
ring note: Fling yourself upon God's providence without making
any reserve whatever—take no thought for the morrow—sell all
you have and give it to the poor—only when the sacrifice is ruth-
less and reckless will the higher safety really arrive.[1]

From Anthony to Francis to Teresa of Ávila, James found a recurring
renunciation of luxury, possessions, and comfort among followers of
Christ. This renunciation, according to James, didn't just happen for the
mere sake of giving something up, but instead was linked to Christlike
love. James found a direct relationship between self-denial and active belief in Christ's love for the world. Consider the following J. J. Chapman
excerpt, which James quotes in his study with approval:

Christ may have meant: If you love mankind absolutely you will
as a result not care for any possessions whatsoever.... If you loved
mankind as Christ loved them, you would see his conclusion as a
fact. It would be obvious. You would sell your goods, and they
would be no loss to you. These truths, while literal to Christ, and
to any mind that has Christ's love for mankind, become parables
to lesser natures.... Thus the whole question of the abandonment
of luxury is no question at all, but a mere incident to another
question, namely, the degree to which we abandon ourselves to
the remorseless logic of our love for others.[2]

Denial of comfort and luxury is a necessary feature of our love for
others. To love another with conviction is to be willing to give up what we
have or what we want.

Even more interestingly, James believed that modern society (which in his time meant the early twentieth century) had tragically lost its vision of the spiritual value of self-denial. In an unusually forceful passage, James offered the following assessment of American culture in 1901:

> Poverty...may...be...the spiritual reform which our time stands most in need of.
>
> Among us English-speaking peoples especially do the praises of poverty need once more to be boldly sung. We have grown literally afraid to be poor. We despise any one who elects to be poor in order to simplify and save his inner life. If he does not join the general scramble and pant with the money-making street, we deem him spiritless and lacking in ambition. We have lost the power even of imagining what the ancient idealization of poverty could have meant: the liberation from material attachments, the unbribed soul...the paying our way by what we are or do and not by what we have, the right to fling away our life at any moment....
>
> Think of the strength which personal indifference to poverty would give us if we were devoted to unpopular causes....
>
> I recommend this matter to your serious pondering, for it is certain that the prevalent fear of poverty among the educated classes is the worst moral disease from which our civilization suffers.[3]

James thought society had forgotten the value of self-denial, of not having rather than having. To not own, according to the "ancient ideal," was to be free, to be unbribed. If James thought this was true of society in 1901, I can only imagine what he might say about us today.

ANTHONY AND THE DESERT FATHERS

Let's swerve back to the third century and the life of Anthony.

Anthony was what you could call the informal Father of the Desert Fathers, the group of early monastics who, before there ever was such a thing as monasticism, famously walked away from society and into the rugged desert of Egypt to pursue a single-minded devotion to the Lord and to their neighbor. It was a life where men were actually treated as equals and where the authority in their lives was the "authority of wisdom, experience, and love."[4]

These hopes might sound somewhat lofty or unrealistic, but the stories and sayings of the Desert Fathers—sayings that beautifully demonstrate humility and a relentless emphasis on love—have inspired centuries of believers, and even today strike the two of us as remarkably relevant.

Richard Foster, in *Freedom of Simplicity,* sums up the Desert Fathers' relevance perfectly:

> They were seeking to revive Christian devotion and simplicity of life by intense renunciation. Their experience has particular relevance, because modern society is uncomfortably like the world that they attacked so vigorously. Their world asked, "How can I get more?" The Desert Fathers [and Mothers] asked, "What can I do without?" Their world asked, "How can I find myself?" The Desert Fathers [and Mothers] asked, "How can I lose myself?" Their world asked, "How can I win friends and influence people?" The Desert Fathers [and Mothers] asked, "How can I love God?"[5]

In Thomas Merton's *The Wisdom of the Desert,* a collection of sayings and stories about the Desert Fathers handed down through the ages, it is evident that the Desert Fathers' idea of love was far from sentimental. Rather, "the full difficulty and magnitude of the task of loving others is recognized everywhere and never minimized," according to Merton. In his view, the Desert Fathers understood that it is very hard for us to love others in the full sense of the word and that it involved "a kind of death of our own being."[6]

The desert, then, wasn't merely a departure from society for the Desert Fathers, but an acknowledgment of the great challenge posed by the love of Christ. The desert wasn't an escape, but an opportunity to accept the gravity of love, and to gradually and truthfully embody the love of Christ in their actual lives.

Anthony was only eighteen years old when the command in Matthew 19:21 struck him so forcibly that he gave away everything—inherited land, possessions—and retreated first to a small village and then the desert. When he emerged twenty years later, as Foster writes, "he was marked with graciousness, love, kindness, endurance, meekness, freedom from anger, and the patience of prayer." Furthermore, "People recognized in him a unique compassion and power."[7]

The curious lives of the Desert Fathers brought them great notoriety, and this was particularly true of Anthony. According to an early biography by Athanasius, even the emperor of Rome (Constantine) and his sons (Constans and Constantius—one has to love the emperor's ego!) wrote to Anthony asking for advice on how to live. Anthony, after being prodded by friends, wrote back only reluctantly and told the emperor not to get puffed up with imperial power, but to make sure to show compassion and take care of the poor.

Interestingly, the people who met Anthony didn't experience a gloomy man who lived a painful, ascetic life, though he certainly was ascetic. They experienced a man who exuded peace and joy, and who pointed them toward a different way of living. People met Anthony and were inspired, sometimes even to leave their lives in order to follow him into the desert.

Strangely, a mass exodus followed Anthony into the desert (one estimate puts the number at fifty thousand). The desert was hot, lonely, dangerous, and isolating, and still whole flocks of people left homes, pools, and status for a life of solitude, discipline, and deprivation, all so they could be free to seek God first and love their neighbor in the fullest sense. As Merton described it, they went not to flee from people but to learn how to find them; not in order to have nothing to do with them, but to find out the way to do them the most good.[8]

And in the minds of the Desert Fathers, finding others meant holding everything they had loosely, in hopes that nothing they owned would hinder their love. Here is one of their pithy sayings:

> Abbot Agatho frequently admonished his disciple, saying: Never acquire for yourself anything that you might hesitate to give to your brother if he asked you for it, for thus you would be found a transgressor of God's command. If anyone asks, give to him, and if anyone wants to borrow from you, do not turn away from him.[9]

Or consider this saying from a Desert Father who understood the strife the *my* and *mine* pronouns can cause.

> There were two elders living together in a cell, and they had never had so much as one quarrel with one another. One therefore said to the other: Come on, let us have at least one quarrel, like other men. The other said: I don't know how to start a quarrel. The first said: I will take this brick and place it here between us. Then I will say: It is mine. After that you will say: It is mine. This is what leads to a dispute and a fight. So then they placed the brick be-

tween them, one said: It is mine, and the other replied to the first:
I do believe that it is mine. The first one said again: It is not
yours, it is mine. So the other answered: Well then, if it is yours,
take it! Thus they did not manage after all to get into a quarrel.[10]

As Christians attempting to know Christ's love today, many of us are
likely quite out of practice when it comes to self-denial. We—and we're
speaking of ourselves here—struggle with sharing even the smallest
things. Self-denial for us means throwing some extra money in the offering plate, or giving up a Saturday at Christmastime to work for a nonprofit, or tossing change into a beggar's cup, but these moments are rarely
more than occasional. Our vision of giving of ourselves seems small and
infrequent by comparison:

> For it was the custom...among...almost all the Egyptian monks
> to hire themselves out at harvest time as harvesters; and each one
> among them would earn eighty measures of corn, more or less,
> and offer the greater part of it to the poor, so that not only were
> the hungry folk of the countryside fed, but ships were sent to
> Alexandria, laden with corn, to be divided among...prisoners...
> or...foreigners.[11]

We aren't telling everyone to run to the caves, but it's hard to not be
convicted by the devotion of the Desert Fathers. Without a doubt, many
later monastics went overboard—whether it was legalistic self-righteousness or a pious cloistering away from the world—and yet the Desert
Fathers themselves continue to strike a chord. While we seek sanctuaries
and houses of worship that match our preferences, the Desert Fathers
walked on foot into the wilderness for a clearer line of sight. While we get
fidgety in long services and bemoan our inability to carve out a regular

time of prayer, the Desert Fathers sought to give the Lord *all* their time, and to realize the love of Christ in everything. The barren wilderness, a life of prayer without ceasing, a relentless commitment to humility, and a love for God and for one's neighbor: these were the Desert Fathers.

LETTING GO OF OUR WILLS

Self-denial and love, then, work together like this: The more we are willing to let go of the tight hold we have on things, the more we question and push back against the desires that control our lives, and the more we open our lives to Christ's control. The less constrained we are by kingdoms of our own making—kingdoms governed by our desires and attachments—the more likely we will mean it when we give up a kingdom of our own making and say "Thy kingdom come," even when it's costly.

This doesn't mean we will necessarily have nothing—as if we could earn God's love by not owning stuff—but rather that we must fundamentally change the way we relate to what we have. It's not about *what* we hold in our hands so much as *how* we hold it, and this cannot be a merely abstract change in posture.

As an example of what it might look like to seek a truthful change in posture, to begin to seek *God's kingdom and His will,* consider this prayer written by French mathematician and philosopher Blaise Pascal:

> Deliver me, Lord,…from the sadness at my proper suffering which
> self-love might give, but put into me a sadness like your own…. I
> ask you neither for health nor for sickness, for life nor for death;
> but that you may dispose of my health and my sickness, my life
> and my death, for your glory, for my salvation, and for the use of
> the Church and of your saints, of whom I would by your grace be
> one. You alone know what is expedient for me; you are the sover-

eign master; do with me according to your will. Give to me, or take away from me, only conform my will to yours. I know but one thing, Lord, that it is good to follow you, and bad to offend you.[12]

Or on a similar note, listen to how Thomas à Kempis summarized the words of Jesus around 1420, in his simple, but profoundly influential book *The Imitation of Christ:*

> Full liberty will never be yours, my son, unless you totally deny yourself. Everyone who seeks and loves only himself is held fast by heavy chains; he is a selfish busybody who always seeks his own interests and not those of Jesus Christ. Whatever he plans or accomplishes will not last long for everything that does not come from God will certainly perish.[13]

Or listen to what John Calvin had to say in his *Golden Booklet of the True Christian Life:* "Show me a single [person] who does not believe in the Lord's law of self-denial who can willingly practice a life of virtue!"[14]

According to Pascal, à Kempis, and Calvin, self-denial was not merely handing over the reins of our lives to God on particular issues. It was a fundamental re-ordering and re-centering of all parts of our lives. We aren't supposed to merely invite Jesus in; we are supposed to uproot and make secondary everything else in the aim of loving Him with all our heart, soul, mind, and strength.

SWIMMING UPSTREAM

Many people throughout our Christian tradition have lived lives of self-denial in the name of Christ. In fact, their lives were so centered on God and His love that denying themselves in some cases became a joyful, willing act that wasn't akin to denial at all but was more an act of love flowing naturally from what was newly alive inside. These Christians understood that self-denial does not require a weary pessimism about attachments or an estrangement from beauty, but rather cheerful satisfaction in God. When they set aside their lives for Christ, they often found a much deeper, more permanent joy on the other side. They lost their lives to gain them. They found that beauty and love are most meaningfully experienced through lives that love God first.

Today, if we expect to follow and live lives transformed by Christ's love, we must be careful to discard, as Tozer said, the pronouns *my* and *mine,* which tend to especially ensnare our hearts. More specifically, as evangelicals whose hopes have frequently been rooted in the fulfillment of marriage, we need to be aware that the *mine* of a longed-for marriage, or the demands we make within marriage, may be one of the most challenging or difficult things to lay down before Him. Even a good gift from Him can become a *mine* all the same.

We should remember that self-denial rarely comes easily or with the approval of the society that surrounds us. The people mentioned above were outliers, people who stood against the social current and provoked their peers to question them as either fools or radicals. They were not products of society but products of a single-minded love and devotion to Christ. Their actions weren't senseless demonstrations of external religion, but the natural fruit of an inward transformation.

Without doubt, there are many Christians today whose love burns brightly with the willingness and vitality of self-denial. Our hope, then, is not to bemoan how our culture has missed the mark in this regard, but simply to encourage us to take Jesus's words seriously and live counterculturally, even if that means rubbing against our own desires and the cultures we've known, so that we might discover more completely what Jesus might be calling us to do in the name of love.

Deep calls to deep
    at the roar of your waterfalls;
all your breakers and your waves
    have gone over me.

By day the LORD commands his steadfast love,
    and at night his song is with me,
    a prayer to the God of my life.

           —Psalm 42:7–8

We will not practice real self-denial unless we fulfill all the duties of love.

    These are not fulfilled by him who merely in an external way performs his services without omitting even one, but by him who acts from a sincere principle of love.

           —John Calvin

I couldn't stop staring at Eli's hands. They looked so handsome on the steering wheel. Reassuring.

As we drove up the coast from Morro Bay to San Francisco, the dramatic vistas of Highway 1 replaced our conversation with jaw-dropping silence. I looked out the driver's window to the ocean cliffs, then to Eli's profile, and then at his hands. There was something about them that encouraged me. Eli was still very much a mystery, but I liked what the West Coast was showing me.

Just a few days before, I had flown out to California to visit Eli, who was spending some time there with friends and family over the holidays. We decided a tour of the sunny West was a better idea than reuniting in Illinois, since it was December after all. It was more fun, but also more complicated, since Eli and I were just friends. Friends always fly across the country to meet another friend's parents around Christmastime, right?

After Eli picked me up from the LA airport, we drove a couple of hours to San Luis Obispo. I was so nervous and jet-lagged that I could hardly finish the burrito that Eli had made a special detour to find for me. Regardless, as we parted the coastal darkness, I felt like Eli and I were starting to hit our stride. Things were comfortable, and my anticipation for the week was high.

When we finally arrived at his parents' vacation home, it was late. I assumed they would be sleeping, but we barely made it through the door before they welcomed me warmly with big hugs and a plate of treats. Suddenly my nerves overtook me—I really wanted these people to like me! I couldn't even take a polite bite of the chocolate chip cookies. Eli enthusiastically introduced me, and I was instantly in love with them. *Yes, these people would make great in-laws,* I thought, then chided myself.

Over the next few days, I was given the grand tour of Eli's life. As expected, Eli's family and friends eyed us suspiciously, wondering who this girl from New York was. My own friends didn't exactly let me hop on the plane without a little bit of hassling, either. Everyone raised eyebrows. Still, Eli and I insisted this was just part of the let's-get-to-know-each-other plan. Sometimes we pulled it off. Sometimes…not so much.

After some lovely days with Eli's family, we continued north to our next destination: San Francisco. Following Highway 1 as it ribboned along the Pacific overhang, we got to know each other better. Our words sometimes found their way and sometimes drifted off. At moments, I leaned out the window, watching the sun ricochet off the cliffs and white-caps. Or I reclined back and tilted my head slightly toward Eli, admiring him. The space between us suddenly felt intimate.

Since my arrival, the trip had been wonderful, even though some-thing just below the surface felt ever so slightly off-kilter. Perhaps it was the discord that came from trying to act like friends when we knew it was more, or maybe it was acting like there could be more when in fact we were just friends. Maybe it was that I couldn't help but let some m-word pressure complicate things. Regardless, during that blissful car ride, any uneasiness vanished and everything finally felt right.

When we arrived in San Francisco, Eli escorted me around, skipping all the unnecessary tourist sites and targeting the locales that he knew I would love. We went to bookstores, museums, special city nooks. We strolled along the water. I met more of his friends, ate Belgian fries, drank salmon beer, and climbed hill after hill. We walked a lot. Almost as much as we talked.

On my last night there, we met up with a group of Eli's friends at one of their favorite spots in the Lower Haight. As the volume increased and the conversations trailed into each other, I experienced the mysterious cord that connects couples across a social gathering. It's that invisible line that causes a girl to stop in the middle of a conversation to meet the eyes of her man who has just glanced over at her. It's that extrasensory string that tugs at a guy's awareness right when his girl needs his attention. It's the connection that joins two people even when they are preoccupied with something else. That night, as I circled around to all of Eli's friends, I had that distinct feeling of being *Eli's* girl. I felt like *we* belonged *together*.

At four o'clock the next morning, I woke up and quietly packed my belongings, careful to not wake Eli's friends, who had been kind enough to open up their apartment to me. Unshowered and tired, I loaded my suitcase into Eli's car and settled into the passenger's seat, a place I had grown very comfortable occupying.

CHAPTER 7

FOCUS OFF THE FAMILY?

So, in the last resort, we must turn down or disqualify our nearest and dearest when they come between us and our obedience to God. Heaven knows, it will seem to them sufficiently like hatred. We must not act on the pity we feel; we must be blind to tears and deaf to pleadings.

—C. S. Lewis

While secularism in the West tends to make an idol out of the individual and his or her needs, traditional religion has often made an idol out of the family.

—Tim Keller

Your mother calls you with the bad news. Before you can even respond, your mind rushes back over a lifetime of memories.

You remember playing catch with your dad in the backyard as you rambled on about dinosaurs and the San Francisco Giants. You remember coming in for dinner after playing in the lot behind your house— where you built forts and dug swimming holes—and your mother would insist on washing the mud off your cheek. In high school, you started a band; your parents attended almost every performance. In college, they helped you pack your belongings into the family car, and your dad carried your things up the campus hill, load by load, into your dorm room. And when you said good-bye to him and your mother in the parking lot behind the dorms, they wept. But college didn't start so well. Your dad counseled you over the phone. He visited regularly and had a new intensity in his eyes. He drove longer distances for even shorter visits. He weathered your new college-inspired ideas and took your new friends to dinner. You returned home for Christmas that year. On the day you arrived, your father left work early, "to kill the fattened calf," he joked. The two of you sat at the kitchen table, together and reunited once again, smiling.

You snap out of your flashbacks to notice your mom is having great difficulty speaking. "Your father had a heart attack," your mother manages to say through her tears.

Now pause and consider the following statement:

> To another he said, "Follow me." But he said, "Lord, let me first go and bury my father." And Jesus said to him, "Leave the dead to bury their own dead. But as for you, go and proclaim the kingdom of God." Yet another said, "I will follow you, Lord, but let me first say farewell to those at my home." Jesus said to him, "No one who puts his hand to the plow and looks back is fit for the kingdom of God." (Luke 9:59–62)

Why would Jesus tell someone not to bury his father?

Our setup is a bit contrived (neither of our fathers have died from a heart attack), but the point is important. When we read the verses in Luke, it's easy to forget that Jesus made these statements to a *real* son, a son who loved his father and who was loved by his father. Imagine your family's shock if you actually did what Jesus told this young man to do, if on the eve of your father's funeral you just walked out of town and left your family behind forever to follow a guy you had only just met. Imagine the outrage and confusion. In one single act, you might sever decades of familial bonds. Extended relatives would be horrified. Friends would wonder whether you were crazy. Your mother and sister would be devastated.

FAMILY MAN

Jesus sounds rather extreme here, doesn't He? What did He mean by such a statement?

To find out, we can't look at just this isolated passage, so let's examine it alongside a few other similar things he said.

> If anyone comes to me and does not hate his own father and mother and wife and children and brothers and sisters, yes, and even his own life, he cannot be my disciple. Whoever does not bear his own cross and come after me cannot be my disciple. (Luke 14:26–27)

And:

> Do not think that I have come to bring peace to the earth. I have not come to bring peace, but a sword. For I have come to set a man against his father, and a daughter against her mother, and a daughter-in-law against her mother-in-law. And a person's enemies will be those of his own household. Whoever loves father or mother more than me is not worthy of me, and whoever loves son or daughter more than me is not worthy of me. And whoever does not take his cross and follow me is not worthy of me. (Matthew 10:34–38)

What does Jesus mean by not "peace, but a sword"? Why would He come to "set a man against his father, and a daughter against her mother?"

These are difficult passages, to be sure, and an improper reading can quickly create significant problems for our communities and families. Read the passages too literally, and one risks harmful or unnecessary chaos in the family, or read the passages too figuratively, and the force of what Jesus said is disregarded. Problems and danger exist on both interpretive sides.

And there are a few more passages that are just as extreme:

> But you are not to be called rabbi, for you have one teacher, and you are all brothers. And call no man your father on earth, for you have one Father, who is in heaven. Neither be called instructors, for you have one instructor, the Christ. (Matthew 23:8–10)

And:

> And his mother and his brothers came, and standing outside they sent to him and called him. And a crowd was sitting around him, and they said to him, "Your mother and your brothers are outside, seeking you." And he answered them, "Who are my mother and my brothers?" And looking about at those who sat around him, he said, "Here are my mother and my brothers! For whoever does the will of God, he is my brother and sister and mother." (Mark 3:31–35)

Again, it feels a bit harsh, doesn't it? And it would have been even more startling if you were part of Jesus's original audience. As New Testament scholar Joseph Hellerman points out, "In the social world of Jewish Palestine, Jesus, as the oldest surviving male in his family (we may presume that His father Joseph had died), was responsible to defend the honor of, and provide leadership for, His patrilineal kinship group."[1] The fact that Jesus said "whoever does the will of God" is His "brother and sister and mother" was especially striking in the context of Jewish culture.

After reading these passages, it seems curious to think that Jesus came in order to nurture Christian families. Christ's emphasis, as you can see, was not quite the same as ours. When Jesus did discuss family, it was often in startling terms. Yet still, "we gravitate toward those portions of the Gospels in which Jesus exhorts His followers to honor their parents or refrain from divorce," Hellerman observes. "Only after we have persuaded ourselves that Jesus is truly family-friendly do we return to the thorny passages cited above and somehow try to fit them into a pro-family reading of the gospels." In other words, he says, "We 'de-fang' the biting edge of Jesus' more radical pronouncements in order to make Jesus safe to take home."[2] Or as theologian Stanley Hauerwas puts it, "The New Testament...seems to have so little to say about sex and marriage. And what it does say has a singularly foreign sound for those of us brought up on romantic notions of marriage and sex."[3]

BIRTHRIGHTS AND BAPTISM

Rather than affirming family as an absolute, Christ frames the kingdom of God in terms of tension and upheaval—hating a wife, setting a daughter against her mother, denying a father. What are we supposed to gather from this? It's difficult to say for sure, of course, and as we've seen, it's dangerous to read the passages too broadly or narrowly.

Nonetheless, at least two explanations seem likely. The first is cultural; Jesus almost certainly wanted to sharpen the distinction between the Jewish concept of family and the kingdom of God. The Jews, of course, valued blood ties. The kingdom of God, however, replaces blood ties with the stronger, albeit less exclusive, ties of faith. The kingdom of

God is built on converts and baptism, not birthrights. A Christian becomes a Christian because he or she has followed Christ. The kingdom
of God, then, is open to everyone. In Christ, there is "neither Jew nor
Greek" (Galatians 3:28), and Jesus's Jewish audience was probably more
likely to understand this if Jesus put it in explicitly anti-familial terms.
The kingdom of God, unlike what came before, meant a new concept of
family. "Whoever does the will of God, he is my brother and sister and
mother" (Mark 3:35).

The second reason is rhetorical; Jesus probably used family-hostile
language to make it clear that discipleship ought to be the absolute most
important thing in our lives. What could be more important than bury-
ing a parent? Following Jesus. What could be worth putting a wife second? Following Jesus. What could be worth giving up your very life?
Following Jesus. Essentially, Jesus arrives in our lives and calls us to follow, then all prior allegiances are rearranged. If Jesus had described discipleship in less radical terms, we probably would have been even more
likely to interpret away the difficulty of what He asked of us.

> For whoever would save his life will lose it, but whoever loses his
> life for my sake will find it. For what will it profit a man if he
> gains the whole world and forfeits his soul? Or what shall a man
> give in return for his soul? (Matthew 16:25–26)

As we thought about Jesus's words, we were reminded of theologian
Dietrich Bonhoeffer's distinction between "cheap grace" and "costly grace":

> Cheap grace is the grace we bestow on ourselves....
>
> Cheap grace is the preaching of forgiveness without requiring
> repentance, baptism without church discipline, communion with-
> out confession.... Cheap grace is grace without discipleship.

Costly grace is the hidden treasure in the field…. It is the
kingly rule of Christ, for whose sake the man will pluck out his
eye that causes him to stumble….

Such grace is *costly* because it calls us to follow, and it is *grace*
because it calls us to follow *Jesus Christ.* It is costly because it
costs us our life, and it is grace because it gives us the only true
life….[4]

And Bonhoeffer continues:

The only man who has the right to say he is justified by grace
alone is the man who has left all to follow Christ. Such a man
knows that the call to discipleship is a gift of grace, and that the
call is inseparable from the grace. But those who try to use this
grace as a[n] [exemption] from following Christ are simply de-
ceiving themselves.[5]

When we overfocus on our own notion of marriage or family, we risk
exchanging a "costly grace," which requires us to follow Christ *first,* for a
"cheap grace" that allows us to cling to our own plans. This is not to say
that marriage and family won't be a huge part of our lives—and a building block of our communities—but rather to remember that we cannot
appropriate His words to our own plans. Again to quote Bonhoeffer:

Humanly speaking, we could understand and interpret the
Sermon on the Mount in a thousand different ways. Jesus knows
only one possibility: simple surrender and obedience, not inter-
preting it or applying it, but doing and obeying it. That is the
only way to hear his word. But again he does not mean that it is
to be discussed as an ideal, he really means us to get on with it.[6]

Following Jesus is about responding to grace in surrender and obedience, even if the surrender and obedience don't always make sense to us.

There is yet another passage in Scripture that might be even more surprising than the rest. It comes at the conclusion of Jesus's conversation with the rich young ruler. After Jesus commands the young man to give away all his possessions—likening a rich man's chance to enter the kingdom to a camel passing through the eye of a needle—the listening crowd is taken aback:

> Those who heard it said, "Then who can be saved?" But [Jesus]
> said, "What is impossible with man is possible with God."... And
> he said to them, "Truly, I say to you, there is no one who has left
> house or wife or brothers or parents or children, for the sake of
> the kingdom of God, who will not receive many times more in
> this time, and in the age to come eternal life." (Luke 18:26–27,
> 29–30)

Here, Jesus actually *promises reward* for the person who has already left his or her family for the kingdom of God. He doesn't tell anyone to leave his or her existing family, but He says those who have left will receive "many times more in this time" and eternal life in the age to come. Shouldn't Jesus have told the family-deserter the opposite?

Now, we don't think Jesus literally calls us to walk away from our families in this passage (see also 1 Timothy 5:8 on the importance of providing for one's family), and we should be extra clear about what we mean here. Jesus doesn't prescribe any particular departure from your family, and no one should take "arbitrary adventures"[7] as Karl Barth put it. But these verses leave little doubt that Jesus must *actually* come first, in the plainest sense of the term. He calls, and we must follow. And if we explain this away too fast, we lose far more than we gain.

The Cost of Discipleship

To most marriage and family experts, the suggestion that a Christian would even consider snubbing family in the name of Christ is lunacy. But if that is so, we suspect they've only halfway dealt with the things Christ said in the Gospels. In our view, Christ was far more interested in forming Christians than Christian families.

> As he said these things, a woman in the crowd raised her voice and said to him, "Blessed is the womb that bore you, and the breasts at which you nursed!" But he said, "Blessed rather are those who hear the word of God and keep it!" (Luke 11:27–28)

To follow Jesus means to truly seek Him before *all* other things, and that emphasis must not be lost on us. Discipleship is about much, much more than raising and protecting a Christian family, or succeeding at family in general. It is about seeking God first, before all things.

Again, Bonhoeffer:

> But the disciples know that the rule is "Seek ye first the kingdom of God and his righteousness, and all these things shall be added unto you." Anxiety for food and clothing is clearly not the same thing as anxiety for the kingdom of God, however much we should like to persuade ourselves that when we are working for our families and concerning ourselves with bread and houses we are thereby building the kingdom, as though the kingdom could be realized only through our worldly cares. The kingdom of God and his righteousness are sharply distinguished from the gifts of the world which come our way. That kingdom is none other than the righteousness of Matt. 5 and 6, the righteousness of the cross

and of following Christ beneath that cross. Fellowship with Jesus and obedience to his commandment come first, and all else follows. Worldly cares are not a part of our discipleship, but distinct and subordinate concerns. Before we start taking thought for our life, our food, our clothing, our work and families, we must seek the righteousness of Christ.[8]

Clearly, following Christ is not a call for the timid: we must lose our lives to gain it, and His call exempts nothing, not even family. "No one who puts his hand to the plow and looks back is fit for the kingdom of God" (Luke 9:62).

> [Jesus assented to God's will]—why? Does he sacrifice himself for others, *yet for his own sake*—in megalomania? Or does he realize himself for the sake of others? The difference is that between a monster and a man. "A new commandment I give unto you: that ye love one another."
>
> —Dag Hammarskjöld

I turned around to look out the window. The wind was lashing at the cold. Inside the coffee shop, customers huddled over their drinks. Winter gear toppled over the benches. We had been lucky to cram ourselves around the only available table, where we sat deep in conversation.

I had expected the weekend to be different. Eli was back in Brooklyn, and I had excitedly awaited his arrival. But my friend Amanda was also there, unexpectedly. Amanda was a friend from college who had called me the night before in tears, heartbroken. Her fiancé had just broken off their engagement. She needed to get away. It just so happened that there were insanely cheap tickets to New York City that weekend, and so when I made the offer for her to come and visit, she jumped on it, and was at my apartment the next morning.

The only glitch was that in a matter of hours after she called, Eli was due to arrive. I was not only excited to see him again, but also had hopes that maybe things would officially move forward with us. However, after Amanda called, my priorities shifted. I called Eli and apologetically explained. He said he would try to adjust his expectations, but I could hear the disappointment in his voice.

In addition to tending my friend's heart, I needed to do laundry, go grocery shopping, and run errands. Real life couldn't be put on complete hold for Eli, and I couldn't afford to treat his visits like a vacation. Not only did I have responsibilities to keep up, but Eli and I needed to interact on real-life terms.

That weekend, doing normal stuff started as a necessity, but slowly grew into something more. As Eli carried my clothes to the laundromat, helped me pick out what to buy for dinner, stood in line with me at the bank, and talked to Amanda about her breakup, surprising vistas of his heart opened up, vistas I wouldn't have been able to see were it not for the real-life scenarios of the weekend.

After a morning of mundane errands, the three of us found ourselves in the nearby coffee shop, cowering from the cold. As we leaned in close over the wobbly table, Eli and I toed the increasingly blurry line between us while Amanda shared her heartache. Eli engaged her, offering her wisdom and the most gentle consolation. It was lovely to watch the exchange. My respect for Eli increased, and suddenly my heart opened up to him with even deeper tenderness. I wanted to claim him as my own, to lay my arm across his shoulder as he talked. But I couldn't. Not yet. I couldn't even explain to Amanda what Eli was coming to mean to me.

When Amanda left the table for a refill, Eli leaned into my ear: "Any interest in taking a stroll?" I looked outside again. Now the wind was splaying the branches of a tree in all directions. Snow flurries had started to fall. Everyone outside was hurrying inside.

"Yes," I replied without hesitation. When Amanda came back, we bundled up and told her we were going to step out for a bit.

We turned down Grand Street and then continued on to Bedford. Even the numbing wind couldn't keep us from a good conversation. We kept plenty of space between us as we walked, though it seemed unnatural, given the cold. We wandered through the neighborhood, taking refuge in a record store. Absent-mindedly, we chatted and flipped through rows of albums while we regained the feeling in our toes.

"Do you think we could get just a little more time alone together this weekend? Just a little?" Eli asked, coming and standing right beside me.

I couldn't fault Eli for the request. Our time was already limited, and neither of us anticipated finding the funds or vacation days for another trip in the near future. We knew these couple days together might be it for a while.

"We can figure something out," I assured him.

Sunday after church, Eli and I finally stole a bit of time for ourselves. We slipped into a café tucked away on the Upper East Side. The place was so tiny, the waitress couldn't walk by without brushing up against the tablecloth. We ordered our food and—I guess feeling the urgency of the moment—Eli immediately started talking.

Surely everyone in the restaurant must have heard our conversation, and I hope they did, because Eli's impromptu speech was really something to be admired. I would have transcribed it, but I was too busy hanging on every word.

Without any rhetorical flourishes, Eli targeted my concerns and laid them to rest. He wooed me with his kindness. He inspired me with his vision of what we could become. And being well aware of my fears, he said I didn't have to decide once and for all whether he was The One. Rather, we could acknowledge that we didn't know—after all, how *could we know?*—and yet we could still move ahead as boyfriend and girlfriend. He didn't have everything figured out, and neither did I, but he believed there was something truly beautiful between us, and that it was worth following into the unknown.

He continued to remind me of what was really important. If things didn't work out, he said, we would still be generous to each other. If I decided he wasn't The One for me, we would still be friends. If he decided the same, it would be okay. We could still be kind. Still be caring. Still think highly of the other. He said with sincerity that he wanted what was best for me, even if it wasn't him. So in addition to taking a new relational step, we also promised that whatever happened in the end, we wouldn't let disappointment trump our commitment to the other's good, even if that felt hard when it came to it. For the time being, we had been given something wonderful, and we should pursue it.

And so, with his characteristic wisdom, Eli quelled my fears and inspired me to enter into a more substantial relationship. He eased my marriage concerns and put our relationship into a new, less fearful perspective. He had won me over. And that was that. We were dating. When we left the restaurant, I happily slipped my arm in his.

We only had the rest of the day to enjoy our new status as boyfriend and girlfriend, since Eli was flying home the next morning. But enjoy it I did. We cooked dinner with Amanda and my roommates, then had friends over for some games. Eli and I sat on the floor, our shoulders touching. I was beaming. Everything felt right. As I continued to lose miserably in the game we were playing, I leaned more comfortably on Eli, happy as could be.

Despite the bustling apartment, everything moved in slow, vibrant strokes. I was surrounded by the people I loved and yet their presence felt different now. It was wonderful to finally see Eli as my boyfriend, but more notably, as a beautiful human being. Wise and lovely. I saw him, as Wendell Berry would say, as a "creature, no more, no less." Momentarily, that night, my heart relaxed.

Walking in the woods. Reading poetry in treetops. Eating brownies on a
candlelit floor. I'm a romantic. Give me a rowboat and I'll find a tranquil
lake to paddle with my lover. Give me a fire escape and I'll have two cups
of tea ready.

A relationship founded on the Internet, then, was a disappointment
to me. I struggled to overcome the banality of how newfangled technol-
ogy had been our first point of contact: my article, Eli's fan e-mail (as I
still like to call it). And it didn't help when Eli's mother explained to her
friends that "They met online." The phrase always made me cringe, not
because meeting online was inferior, but simply because it wasn't the
story I had imagined for myself—one full of bashful glances, face-to-face
laughter, accidental touches. Add to that disappointment the miles between us, and my sentimental heart was desperate for a little more color,
intimacy, romance!

Instead, I got e-mails. And phone calls. And the occasional visit.
These things were nice, but limiting. We tried to compensate, but the
ordinary was always missing. That quick drink after a long day of work.
That good-bye kiss that was only meant to last the night. The spontaneous stroll or show or party. The mutual friends and churches and experiences. *Seeing* each other. We didn't have that.

Long distance was a drag. Sure, you spend a lot of time talking and
getting to know each other, but you don't really get to know each other
beyond what you each choose to reveal. There is so much more to a person than what can be expressed in a phone call or e-mail. The Internet
definitely made things easier, in some regards, but I could never quite
make peace with how darn *modern* our tale was. I would have preferred

things a little more old-fashioned, but that would have meant no Eli in the first place.

So things were not ideal, but at least we had found each other, even if we did so under less-than-perfect conditions. And Eli certainly found ways to add a little spark. I remember a slideshow presentation he sent me to share a trip he had gone on. It included a photo of him looking at the camera with a snowflake adorning his mustache. His expression alone kept my heart thudding. I also remember a card he made. He had stolen (borrowed?) the *Connect-Four* pieces from his favorite coffee shop and taken them out to the sidewalk where he spelled my name with them and took photos. Then he pasted the photos inside the card. "You are a lovely surprise," he wrote. Another time he surprised me by having a darling plant in a green pot delivered to me at my office. These whimsical touches helped get us through our weeks of separation.

But I struggled all the same. Perhaps what was most disconcerting was not when the relationship felt hard, but when it felt easy, when my life was so separate from Eli's that I bounced from week to week effortlessly, keeping Eli in a compartment that had little impact on my day-to-day activities. Then when we *did* see each other, I was jolted, having to adjust to the real-life Eli, not the virtual one my imagination had so carefully groomed and edited. By the time I got used to him, Eli and I would part ways again. Trying to form, not simply maintain, a relationship over telephone wires and broadband was like trying to build a sandcastle. Rather than my affections for Eli cementing, they kept shifting.

I knew there was something special between us, but when I couldn't feel it while cooking dinner on a weeknight, it was hard to believe it really existed.

When it says "all your heart, all your soul, all your mind," it leaves no part of our life free from this obligation, no part free as it were to back out and enjoy some other thing; any other object of love that enters the mind should be swept towards the same destination as that to which the whole flood of our love is directed. So a person who loves his neighbour properly should, in concert with him, aim to love God with all his heart, all his soul, and all his mind. In this way, loving him as he would himself, he relates his love of himself and his neighbour entirely to the love of God, which allows not the slightest trickle to flow away from it and thereby diminish it.

—Augustine

CHAPTER 8

THE LOST CHAPTER

And surely St. Paul is right? If I may trust my own experience, it is (within marriage as without) the practical and prudential cares of this world, and even the smallest prosaic of those cares, that are the great distraction.

—C. S. Lewis

What do I have when I won't let go? The question burrowed deep into our brains.

Theologians had said it for centuries now, and there was little we could add to their chorus. We can hold our attachments freely as gifts given by Him, or our attachments can hold us.

But why should attachments matter in the first place? Why do theologians harp on them?

One reason, of course—not likely to be a surprise—is love, that is, a love for God and for one's neighbor. These luminous loves form the center of our grace-inspired lives in Him. We receive grace, and we respond in an upward motion of obedience that gradually replaces the life we knew before. Love is the outflow and fruit of a life changed by grace.

This upward motion implies a downward corollary: Any earthly attachment we find and cling to can be a division of what Christ said should be our first loves. Potential attachments, we know, include the obvious stuff: money, fame, power, possessions. But even noble jobs, dear friendships, and good deeds can become attachments if they aren't grounded in true love for God. Without love, 1 Corinthians 13 tells us, we gain nothing.

And 1 Corinthians says something else as well: Relationships, even church-sanctioned ones, can be attachments, capable of dividing our attention from God. While that might sound dour, it was Paul who suggested it first. In chapter 7, Paul laid out a careful treatment of marriage and singleness, directly exploring the danger posed by the beautiful provision God laid out for man in Genesis 2.

To be honest, we think that if we took Paul's treatment a bit more seriously, we likely wouldn't need a book like this. But the fact is, we don't take 1 Corinthians 7 very seriously. We often don't even acknowledge it's there, which is odd, since 1 Corinthians as a whole has a comfortable presence in the pulpit. We hear lots about 1 Corinthians 5 and 6 (avoiding sexual immorality), and we memorize 1 Corinthians 13 (love, generally); but we seem to have forgotten about the bulk of chapter 7, in which Paul essentially commends and recommends singleness. We find it strange that *these* verses are the ones neglected, given how much time the church generally spends on the topic of sex and relationships.

In fact, 1 Corinthians 7 is the most direct comparative treatment of singleness and marriage in the Bible, and yet it is absent from most sermons on marriage. And still, it seems to be spoken of only rarely in the sprawling complex of Christian marriage and family literature. Of course, other verses in the Bible address marriage—Genesis 1 and 2 and Ephesians 5, most notably—and other topics have implications for singleness (like the elder requirements in 1 Timothy and Titus), but no other passage in the Bible considers the two statuses so explicitly in relation to each other. Certainly, then, a recommendation to remain single (specifically compared to marriage) has implications for our understanding of marriage, right?

So let's look at a passage from 1 Corinthians 7, particularly verses 25–40, and then consider what it says.

Now concerning the betrothed, I have no command from the Lord, but I give my judgment as one who by the Lord's mercy is trustworthy. I think that in view of the present distress it is good for a person to remain as he is. Are you bound to a wife? Do not seek to be free. Are you free from a wife? Do not seek a wife. But if you do marry, you have not sinned, and if a betrothed woman marries, she has not sinned. Yet those who marry will have worldly troubles, and I would spare you that. This is what I mean, brothers: the appointed time has grown very short. From now on, let those who have wives live as though they had none, and those who mourn as though they were not mourning, and those who rejoice as though they were not rejoicing, and those who buy as though they had no goods, and those who deal with the world as though they had no dealings with it. For the present form of this world is passing away.

I want you to be free from anxieties. The unmarried man is anxious about the things of the Lord, how to please the Lord. But the married man is anxious about worldly things, how to please his wife, and his interests are divided. And the unmarried or betrothed woman is anxious about the things of the Lord, how to be holy in body and spirit. But the married woman is anxious about worldly things, how to please her husband. I say this for your own benefit, not to lay any restraint upon you, but to promote good order and to secure your undivided devotion to the Lord.

If anyone thinks that he is not behaving properly toward his betrothed, if his passions are strong, and it has to be, let him do as he wishes: let them marry—it is no sin. But whoever is firmly established in his heart, being under no necessity but having his desire under control, and has determined this in his heart, to keep her as his betrothed, he will do well. So then he who marries his betrothed does well, and he who refrains from marriage will do even better.

A wife is bound to her husband as long as he lives. But if her husband dies, she is free to be married to whom she wishes, only in the Lord. Yet in my judgment she is happier if she remains as she is. And I think that I too have the Spirit of God.

Interesting, right? Now let's look at the two primary things Paul says about singleness and marriage.

A RECOMMENDATION

First, Paul recommends singleness over marriage. In verse 7, Paul says, "I wish that all were as I myself am," meaning single. In verse 8, he repeats the statement: "To the unmarried and the widows I say that it is good for them to remain single as I am." He keeps going: "Are you free from a wife? Do not seek a wife" (verse 27).

Paul is careful to make it clear that these are not rigid commands. Lest they be taken to the opposite extreme—as they often have in the history of the church—Paul explains that "if you do marry, you have not sinned" (verse 28). Further, he is aware and careful to recognize that sexual sin is a destructive force, and so even while he recommends singleness, he thinks it would be better to get married than be dismantled by simmering temptation.

Everything Paul says here is neatly consistent with Jesus's discussion

of singleness in Matthew 19. In that chapter, Jesus acknowledges and approves of those who choose singleness for the sake of the kingdom of
heaven, saying, "Let the one who is able to receive this [singleness] receive
it" (verse 12). Like Paul, Jesus points out that not everyone will be able to
handle this situation—"let the one who is able"—but for those who can
handle it, Jesus approves.

DIVIDED ATTENTION

Second, Paul ties his recommendation for singleness to a reason: The
married person runs the risk of dividing his or her attention from God. If
your experience was like ours, you didn't hear this. Marriage was an opportunity to be blessed, to be sanctified, and to love sacrificially. But
marriage as a distraction from God? The idea was rarely aired.

Indeed, it is difficult to escape the conclusion that Paul's advice here
runs against a substantial portion of the advice shared by many Christian
marriage experts. Paul clearly doesn't say a Christian can't pursue God
and a spouse at the same time, but he does say a spouse can keep us from
wholly seeking God's approval. Paul calls husbands to love their wives as
Christ loved the church, but he also encourages Christians to stay single
if they can handle it. Neither exhortation should be ignored, and yet we
can't consider them in light of each other if we pretend one doesn't exist.

To put it another way, even if we believe the average Christian can't
handle singleness—as many in the church seem to—we should still remind the few that *can* handle it that singleness is biblically described as a
path that *helps* people to focus on God, not one that hinders or marginal-
izes them. And we shouldn't merely mouth these words as an afterthought, as a gesture of patronage, but the words should be repeated until
our lives reflect some confirmation of their truth. And in a culture like
ours, this might be much more difficult than it sounds.

Now, clearly singleness does not *automatically* help a person focus on God. All of us can cite many, many instances of selfish, immature singles: bachelors and bachelorettes without obligations who remain crassly protective of their time and freedom. The single person who is able to focus attention toward God and yet uses freedom selfishly squanders the very opportunity Paul holds up as a good. And yet that potential for selfishness should not change the sense that it is indeed a good thing.

Matthew Henry summed up the idea nicely in his eighteenth-century commentary:

> Celibacy is not in itself a state of greater purity and sanctity than marriage; but the unmarried would be able to make religion more their business at that juncture, because they would have less distraction from worldly cares. Marriage is that condition of life that brings care along with it, though sometimes it brings more than at others.[1]

And Augustine said something quite similar in the fifth century: "We do not praise the fact that they [single people] are [single], but that they are dedicated to God."[2] Singleness on its own is no guarantee that we will give what we have to God, and yet that doesn't provide a reason to ignore the fact that it is marriage that Paul describes as a point of division. Even if we long for a culture that better respects the lifelong commitment of marriage, we should not ignore its potential to divide.

Chapter Six Is for You. Chapter Seven? Eh, Not so Much.

As we said before, we generally tend to highlight 1 Corinthians 6 because of its helpful treatment of sexual ethics (the body is a "temple of the

Holy Spirit," verse 19), but once we turn to chapter 7, many of us begin to squirm. We either muffle the difficult stuff in the name of textual complexity, afraid to acknowledge that marriage is "neither a means of enhancing one's status nor required for the purpose of preserving the social cosmos,"[3] to use Barry Danylak's words. Or we mute the chapter by turning it into a complicated cultural matter we couldn't possibly understand. As Stanley Hauerwas put it, "Attempt[s] to rescue the New Testament views on marriage and sexuality seem to involve creative forms of exegesis."[4]

We'll breeze through two quick examples of this. First, some people argue that the meaning of chapter 7 is contingent on Paul's circumstances, on his "present distress" (verse 26), and thus is not applicable for us today. While it is impossible to know exactly what Paul meant by this statement, most commentaries suggest that Paul's recommendation is in fact for *everyone*. To quote one:

> There are some, however, that view the term *"necessity"* as referring to the age of the Apostle, which was, undoubtedly, full of trouble to the pious: but he appears to me to have had it rather in view to express the disquietude with which the saints are incessantly harassed in the present life. I view it, therefore, as extending to all ages, and I understand it in this way, that the saints are often, in this world, driven hither and thither, and are exposed to many and various tempests, so that their condition appears to be unsuitable for marriage. The phrase *"so to be,"* signifies to remain unmarried, or to abstain from marriage.[5]

That was Calvin. Or consider contemporary scholar Craig Blomberg, who interprets the "distress" in the passage as the tension all Christians feel in light of the uncertainty of the end of time: "If we are correct in seeing verses 29–31 as…[describing] the characteristic tension believers experience between the two advents of Christ, then Paul's counsel remains equally valid for any time and place throughout church history."[6]

I, Not the Lord

Second, others have suggested that Paul's statements about singleness aren't for everyone because, in verses 12 and 25, Paul says they are his words and not the Lord's. Likewise, in verse 6, Paul prefaces his recommendation to stay single with a note that the statement is a "concession," not a "command."

These verses clearly soften the rigidness of Paul's recommendation, and we likewise want to avoid any sort of legalism. But even so, a majority of commentaries argue that the chapter is not to be ignored due to the qualification. Here's Matthew Henry again: [This statement] "is worded with modesty, but delivered, notwithstanding, with apostolic authority. It is not the mere opinion of a private man, but the very determination of the Spirit of God in an apostle, though it be thus spoken."[7]

In other words, according to Henry, just because Paul says, "I, not the Lord," it doesn't mean his words aren't inspired or to be taken less seriously.

And John Wesley agrees. In his commentary on 7:25, he writes:

[Paul had] no commandment from the Lord—by a particular revelation. Nor was it necessary he should; for the apostles wrote nothing which was not divinely inspired. But with this difference; sometimes they had a particular revelation, and a special commandment; at other times they wrote from the divine light which abode with them, the standing treasure of the Spirit of God. And this also was not their private opinion, but a divine rule of faith and practice.[8]

We hope these quick discussions have helped shed a little light on 1 Corinthians 7 and the notion that we shouldn't be so quick to ignore the chapter. Neither the "present distress" argument nor the "I, not the Lord" argument alters Paul's recommendation for singleness.

A More Complete Conversation

In light of this, then, a proposal: The next time we talk about marriage, let's talk about 1 Corinthians 7 as well. It sounds simple, but it might help our discussion. Sure, we should talk about how marriage can reflect Christ's love for the church, but let's also talk about how marriage can divide our attention from God. Rather than talk only about how marriage helps us grow, let's also talk about what it means to be torn between pleasing a spouse and pleasing God. We might only be better for having had the conversation.

The same day Sadducees came to him, who say that there is no resurrection, and they asked him a question, saying, "Teacher, Moses said, 'If a man dies having no children, his brother must marry the widow and raise up offspring for his brother.' Now there were seven brothers among us. The first married and died, and having no offspring left his wife to his brother. So too the second and third, down to the seventh. After them all, the woman died. In the resurrection, therefore, of the seven, whose wife will she be? For they all had her."

But Jesus answered them, "You are wrong, because you know neither the Scriptures nor the power of God. For in the resurrection they neither marry nor are given in marriage, but are like angels in heaven. And as for the resurrection of the dead, have you not read what was said to you by God: 'I am the God of Abraham, and the God of Isaac, and the God of Jacob'? He is not God of the dead, but of the living." And when the crowd heard it, they were astonished at his teaching.

—Matthew 22:23–33

Whom have I in heaven but you?
    And there is nothing on earth that I desire besides you.
My flesh and my heart may fail,
    but God is the strength of my heart and my portion forever.

—Psalm 73:25–26

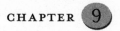

CHAPTER 9

TIPS FROM TOLSTOY

And we are put on earth a little space,
That we may learn to bear the beams of love.

—William Blake

"Marriage teaches you to be *less* selfish," I heard when I was younger. Often the person who told me this would go on to explain: In the normal state of things, we are selfish people plagued by selfish habits. But! Marriage stems that somewhat. By navigating life with another, marriage channels our selfish impulses into something better; we learn to become more generous by being forced to take into account the preferences and needs of another.

Surely, there is much truth in this, and the idea made sense to me not only in a practical sense, but biblically, too. Husbands were to love their wives as Christ loved the church (see Ephesians 5:25), and this required sacrifice that brought about sanctification, a process of becoming more like Christ through the often painful process of moving beyond selfish habits. Maintaining a marriage would be difficult at times, and working through the challenges was one way of bringing us up and out of our selves.

I liked this idea because it placed the struggles I had seen into a constructive context. When couples I knew fought, it wasn't just chaos, but something more significant. As someone who wanted to get married, I liked that this both accounted for a couple's inevitable disagreements and infused the conflicts with meaning in the grander scheme of things.

There was some variation in what I heard on this topic from church to church, and yet overall there was a fairly consistent understanding that marriage was largely (or maybe even entirely) swept up in the work of sanctification. If you wanted to get serious about growing, you got married. Sanctification happened in other places, too, but it *especially* happened in marriage.

And yet as I got older, something about this explanation didn't sit right with me. In the marriages I had seen thus far, I was finding it increasingly difficult to see all events as sanctification. I had certainly seen some amazing spouses and some beautiful acts of generosity, but I had seen quite a bit of other stuff, too.

For example, I had seen couples with noncomplementary career goals, couples that for the sake of children or family had to choose one career or the other, but not both. Sometimes this decision went well, but sometimes it poisoned everything with resentment, even in Christian marriages. I had seen friends with vastly different views on money: how much it should be sought, how it should be spent, and how it could or should be shared. Sometimes one spouse would bring the other over to a shared view, but sometimes disagreements became intractable—two strong visions with little hope for reconciliation. I had also seen couples with vastly differing degrees of ambition. I had seen spouses gracefully accept their less ambitious spouses, in spite of dreams that may have been left behind, but I had also seen heartbreaking manipulation and control, a spirit-crushing unwillingness to extend grace toward someone who wasn't quite as successful as what had been envisioned in The Plan. These dynamics were not confined to just marriage, of course, but when I was feeling less optimistic, marriage seemed like an especially fruitful breeding ground for these patterns. The divorce rate was staggering, and I was starting to feel like I could see why, even among Christians. Where was the sanctification I had heard about?

I knew that no relationship was perfect, and that included nonmarital relationships, but it felt like at least some amount of what I'd seen in the marriages around me wasn't so much growth in holiness but something else. There was clearly beauty to be found in their struggles, because we all grow through loving the difficult and sacrificing ourselves. But at other points I couldn't see much beauty at all and very little sacrifice. Sometimes the marriages looked more like a protracted cage match, a struggle for power and freedom in a newly confined space.

Was this fighting always to be thought of as sanctification? Was the mere existence of a struggle between married Christians enough to imply that sanctification was happening? Clearly I couldn't answer these questions for other people, nor was I the one who ultimately knew what was and wasn't sanctification, but I wanted to know for the sake of my own approach to marriage. I wanted to believe that the relational challenges I had seen were working out for the good of my friends, and would ultimately work out for my good once I got married, but I couldn't escape the fact that there was a great deal in what I saw that looked more like chaos than growth, like sparks flying up after a clashing of swords.

I was comfortable with the idea that disagreements would be present in any deep relationship, but I wanted those disagreements to be *toward God,* not *away from God.* I didn't want to risk calling something "sanctification" that really wasn't. Paul had said pleasing a spouse was not always the same thing as pleasing God (see 1 Corinthians 7), and yet I felt like I could hardly say what that meant in practice. In essence, I wanted to love a spouse the way Christ loved the church (see Ephesians 5), but I didn't want to be caught up and distracted in the work of pleasing a spouse. How was I to know which was which?

TIPS FROM TOLSTOY

While I was thinking about this, I was reminded of a graph a friend showed me, a graph drawn by none other than Count Leo Tolstoy, the cranky Russian novelist who wrote *Anna Karenina, War and Peace, The Death of Ivan Ilyich,* and many other works.

The story behind the graph goes like this. Apparently one day Ilya Tolstoy, the son of Count Leo, had written a letter to his bride-to-be (Tanya). Tolstoy, like your average concerned parent, intercepted the letter somehow (we don't know why) and decided that he should write Ilya a letter in return. Tolstoy said he had been thinking about his son's impending marriage a great deal, "with joy and with fear, mixed," and he wanted to share a few tips with his son before the big day.

A paragon of clear communication, Tolstoy decided a quick pair of graphs would help him make his point. Here's essentially what the first graph looked like:

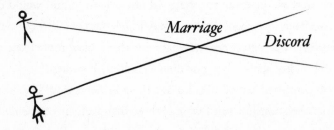

"This is what I think…" Tolstoy wrote. "If one marries in order to enjoy oneself more, no good will ever come of it. To set up as one's main object, ousting everything else, marriage, union with the being you love, is a great mistake."[1]

This seemed like a bold statement when I first read it. According to Tolstoy, not one to mince words, the mistake was "an obvious one." Why? "Well, you marry; and what then? If you had no other object in life before your marriage, it will be twice as fearfully hard, almost impossible, to find one. In fact you may be sure, if you had no common purpose before your marriage, nothing can bring you together, you will keep getting further apart. Marriage can never bring happiness unless those who marry have a common purpose."[2] The point of the graph then was to demonstrate this: If no purpose exists outside yourself, your own selfishness (and the selfishness of your spouse) will naturally and gradually create ever-increasing distance, and the distance will eventually result in mounting strife and discord.

Now, I'm not sure the less-than-orthodox Tolstoy is generally the guy you want to turn to for advice. The Count had a tortured final decade with his wife—she once fired a gun at him, only missing him narrowly, and he wrote terribly dark short stories about her—but I couldn't help but wonder if he had a point here.

The other alternative, Tolstoy wrote his son, was that you had a purpose *outside of yourself.* In that case, things would look like this:

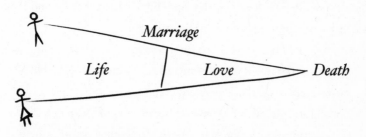

This is how the Count explained the second graph:

Your purpose in life must not be to enjoy the delight of wedlock but, by your life, to bring more love and truth into the world. The object of marriage is to help one another in the attainment of that purpose.

The vilest and most selfish life is the life of the people who have joined together only in order to enjoy life; and the highest vocation in the world is that of those who live in order to serve God by bringing good into the world, and who have joined together for that express purpose. Don't mistake half-measures for the real thing. Why should a man not choose the highest? Only, when you have chosen the highest, you must set your whole heart on it and not just a little. Just a little leads to nothing. There, I am tired of writing and still have much left that I wanted to say. I kiss you.[3]

In Tolstoy's view, then, if the purpose was love, two spouses wouldn't grow more separate as they tried to reconcile self-directed paths, but would rather be drawn closer as they lived a life of service to God, that is, as they approached love. If the path wasn't confined to personal fulfillment, there would be less discord and perhaps more fulfillment in the end.

Soon after I read Tolstoy, I stumbled upon another little excerpt—this one written a few decades ago by Richard Foster and Dallas Willard—that basically echoed the same idea.

The New Testament regards romantic love as such a negligible factor in marriage that it does not even *mention* it. Disciples can no longer neglect this form of love because in our world of today it is running amuck destroying the lives of millions by its insubordination to *agape* [love]. Disciples must, above all, be convinced and must convince their children that people *cannot* build a marriage upon either sexual attraction or romantic love alone and that the goodness which is in these is available *only* within properly *agapized* homes and communities. The basis of the Christly marriage and family is *mutual* subordination to the good of others out of a respect for Christ (Eph. 5:21).[4]

This, then, I thought was perhaps the beginning of a response to my earlier question. How was I to know the difference between a sanctifying struggle (see Ephesians 5) and a struggle that would distract me from God (see 1 Corinthians 7)?

Maybe the difference was love.

Better is a dinner of herbs where love is than a fattened ox and hatred with it.

—Proverbs 15:17

WHAT WOULD IT MEAN?

Humanity was sleeping—it is still sleeping—imprisoned
in the narrow joys of its little closed loves.

—Pierre Teilhard de Chardin

My friend was beaming. I rarely saw him decked out in anything more
than jeans and a tattered shirt, but he was looking nothing short of re-
spectable in his tux. And when I noted the warmth in his eyes as he
focused on his wife-to-be, I was struck by the beautiful significance of
the day.

The groom was an old college roommate of mine, a dear friend
and longtime fellow musician (a drummer—think Animal from The
Muppets). He and I had shared no shortage of great times over the years:
endless debates about the Foo Fighters, an unholy love of Cheez-Its,
and about ten weeks on the road in a cramped RV opening for the
Hanson brothers.

To say the least, the friendship was an inspired one, charmed from
the beginning with laughter and an absurd streak of shared experiences.

I couldn't have been more excited about his big day. My friend had
found a terrific girl. She was engaging, humble, kind, articulate, beautiful—all the things you hope for in a teammate. She loved Jesus deeply,

and the love in her life flowed naturally into her relationships and the way she treated those around her. She was worthy of my friend in every way.

As a groomsman on the wedding day, I stood by their side with great delight. Everything felt like it was in its right place, and I felt a swelling gratitude. I loved being with them when they were together, and so the big day felt like a precursor for more good times to come. Notably absent in my heart was any sense of fear or reservation. Certainly my friend and his bride would face their challenges, like all couples do, and yet they seemed to be starting on solid ground.

I shuffled my feet, to keep my emotions back as the moment overwhelmed me. And then the minister began to read 1 Corinthians 13:

> Love is patient and kind; love does not envy or boast; it is not arrogant or rude. It does not insist on its own way; it is not irritable or resentful; it does not rejoice at wrongdoing, but rejoices with the truth. Love bears all things, believes all things, hopes all things, endures all things. *Love never ends.* (verses 4–8)

I had heard these verses countless times during my childhood, and yet suddenly the verses felt alive. They resonated within my heart. How beautiful a picture this was! How compelling a vision! It's no wonder why this chapter commends itself to our most solemn and hopeful gatherings.

And truly, it was delightful to think of my dear friend and his bride working this out in the new union of their lives. They would learn patience through their impatience, kindness through their unkindness, humility through their tendency to be prideful. They would learn to bear all things through the challenge of bearing hard things. They would learn to hope through the propensity to doubt. They would mirror one to another and would provoke great growth in each other's lives.

FOR ALL

Paul's meditation on love in 1 Corinthians 13 is a stunning set of exhortations, and it's no surprise to me why the chapter has inspired so many people; it is a breathtaking picture of the beauty and completeness of love.

And yet even as we admire it, we can also remind ourselves that the chapter is not only for marriage. We can admire the beauty of love in one context, yet not forget its relevance elsewhere. Yes, 1 Corinthians 13 was a beautiful catalyst for my friend and his bride, and is for any couple who seeks to saturate their lives with it. We should teach, hope, and nurture this in marriages without hesitancy.

But the spark of 1 Corinthians 13 is also for the totality of who we are. Our marriages should not be a singular instance of love in our lives, but one more outpouring of an inward reality transformed. Our coworkers, our bosses, our siblings, ruling authorities, political foes, parents, enemies, and the stranger on the side of the road: the love of Christ is for them as well. We know only a skeleton of love if it doesn't engulf the whole.

Many of us know this, and yet I'm not sure we knead it into our lives. We might agree with it on paper, but we shrink back when it places a demand on us. "We are already stretched too thin," we might say. Or "that coworker is the least of my worries."

It is easier to speak of love than to move into it, and I say all this as someone who knows it all too well. I pontificate with the best, and yet my words evaporate in the face of a person who will truly cost me something.

In view of that, then, here is a list of questions drawn from 1 Corinthians 13, a list I hope to grow into as I grow into grace. They aren't rocket science, and one could quickly think of a hundred more. I tried to choose topics that I personally lose sight of.

- As friends, what would 1 Corinthians 13 mean for our relational pettiness? How would we relate to others if we were patient and

kind? Would we speak ill of others when they weren't around?
Would we hold grudges when others wrong us? What might
patience mean for the way we listen?

- As congregations, what would 1 Corinthians 13 mean for our
  clamoring struggle for influence, our need to be known and
  thought well of? What would it mean for pastors who seek
  to build their platform and for us as congregants who seek to
  exercise authority over others? What would it mean to live in
  communities that truly didn't envy or boast?

- What would 1 Corinthians 13 mean to the invisible boundaries
  that divide our churches, the wealthy associating with the
  wealthy, and the influential with the influential? Does not
  Christ's love cover human distinction, as Christ did among the
  poor, the sick, the blind, the sinner, and *the least of these*?

- As employees, what would it mean to be patient and kind rather
  than arrogant or rude? As employers, what would it mean to
  endure all things, to bear all things, to hope for all things?

- As strangers, what would it mean to be kind when we encounter
  someone on the street? Are we to be kind only when we find true
  need, when we find someone who won't squander what we give?
  Or are we to be kind to all? Are we to pass by hurriedly, or are
  we to give to those who ask? Love need not create a foolish
  martyr, and yet love *endures all things*.

- As children, what would it mean to not insist on our own way,
  to not become irritable or resentful? What if we gave up the
  anger and resentment that clutter and poison our interior lives?
  What would it mean to let go in view of the forgiveness of
  Christ, to forgive as we ourselves have been forgiven?

- As disciples, what would change if we sought the fullness of His
  love?

The dark truth is that we may praise love,…and few people would refuse to do so when love is rightly understood. We may wish to be loving—to be kind and helpful in our relations to those near to us. But we do not trust love, and we think it could easily ruin our carefully guarded hold on life.…

Above all, one has to find by thought and experience that love can be trusted as a way of life. This can be learned by interaction with Jesus in all ordinary and extraordinary circumstances.… He can bring it to pass that we rely on love; and that is why he boldly asserted that the *only* mark of being his student or apprentice in life was how his students love one another (John 13:35). And it is, again, why one of his best students could say, on the basis of a lifetime of experience: "Everyone who loves is born of God and knows God" (1 John 4:7). Love is not God, but God is love. It is who he is, his very identity. And our world under a God like that is a place where it is safe to do and be what is good and what is right. Living in love as Jesus defines it by his words and deeds is the sure way to know Christ in the modern world. On the other hand, if you are not reconciled to living in love as the center of your life, and *actually* living that way, any knowledge you may have of Christ will be shallow and shaky at best.

—Dallas Willard

I felt a tap on my shoulder. I turned around to see a woman with messy hair and mismatched clothes. I looked at her suspiciously, half expecting her to ask me for money.

"Would you mind if I prayed for you?" she asked instead.

New York was shivering with winter's cold. I had ducked inside the sanctuary of St. Luke in the Fields for an afternoon break. During the winter, my options for a midday escape from the office were limited, so I got in the habit of eating my sandwich quickly at my desk and bundling up for a brisk walk up the street to St. Luke's. This stunning chapel in the West Village was always welcoming, leaving its doors open to anyone who needed a quiet place to rest. I wish I could say I was drawn to its bright sanctuary out of piety, but the attraction was primarily because it offered a warm seat where I could be alone and take my mind off work for a little while.

On this afternoon, as on many others, the sun streamed through the tall stained-glass windows onto the wooden pews. I sat in the empty church, cloistered from the noise of the city, and prayed. I prayed about one thing: Eli. I spent many hours in that church begging God for guidance and clarity regarding my relationship with him.

With my coat still buttoned and my scarf still wrapped, I sat hunched over my Bible, hoping to discover clues that would give me a glimpse into my future and whether or not it should include Eli. I prayed and I pleaded. I read and I meditated. And all along, I was oblivious to the single dimension of my desires. I was too busy treating God like a matchmaker to realize that I was hardly seeking God at all. Though I prayed, rather earnestly, for His will to be done, I was really only seeking a path free of heartache. I just wanted to know if I should marry Eli or if it was all a waste of time.

Dietrich Bonhoeffer spoke of a single-minded obedience to God, a simple obedience that includes all things. If we are true disciples, then we are to seek God truly first, before all else. My anxiousness over marriage—even though it was often directed toward God—had slowly edged Him out as my focal point. Somehow, without even knowing it, I had reduced God to a means.

I knew that we cannot serve two masters, but I thought this only applied to money and success and other modern idols. Never had it occurred to me that marriage could become a master in my life and one I sought religiously. For this reason, I didn't even notice how it consumed my interior life, dominated my prayers. Or, as Bonhoeffer might say, I didn't see that marriage had put a barrier between me and my true master.

If I had understood what it meant to follow Christ single-mindedly, I would have entered St. Luke's that day to seek God and God alone. I would have still talked to Him about Eli and my future, and there would be nothing wrong with that, but clarity regarding Eli would not have been my main motivation. My error that day was not in praying about the relationship; it was in seeking a marriage from God rather than seeking God.

Basically, I wanted my happy ending and I was growing impatient. I had forgotten the value of unresolved suspense. This reminded me of another thing Bonhoeffer said:

> If it is I who determine where God is to be found, then I shall always find a God who corresponds to me in some way, who is obliging, who is connected with my own nature. But if God determines where he is to be found, then it will be in a place which

is not immediately pleasing to my nature and which is not at all congenial to me. This place is the Cross of Christ. And whoever would find him must go to the foot of the Cross, as the Sermon on the Mount commands. This is not according to our nature at all, it is entirely contrary to it. But this is the message of the Bible, not only in the New but also in the Old Testament.[1]

I was looking for God in a happy ending, an ending where all would be resolved. I had forgotten that sometimes God's ways are anything but congenial to me, though they are always better. I had forgotten that the Christian life does not always reside in a neat ending, though surely we have a great conclusion to look forward to. Sometimes God is found in the three days when Christ was in the tomb, or in the despair of Psalm 88 or in the uncertainty that Lamentations hangs on (see 5:22). Sometimes, we experience God in the unhappy tension, the prayer cut off mid-supplication, the hope interrupted with an ellipsis. Sometimes God prefers to work with the unraveled end instead of a tidy bow, because that can be how we learn to linger in the uncertainty of faith.

Sitting in St. Luke's, however, I did not want to linger. I wanted God to get me to my resolution. I had not learned patience or single-minded discipleship. I was still trying to determine where God could be found. So that afternoon, God tried to set me straight.

"Would you mind if I prayed for you?" the woman asked again.

"Um, sure," I muttered uncomfortably.

She put her hands on my shoulders and started to pray passionately, sometimes in English and sometimes in Spanish. She prayed and she prayed. I was deeply moved. Then near the end of her prayer, she began to pray for my future husband—or really she prayed that I not be anxious about my future husband for the Lord would make it clear. I was shocked by her intuition! How had she known?

When she finished, I didn't know what to do. I chatted with her awkwardly for a few seconds, still surprised by what had happened. Then I said a quick good-bye and hurriedly walked back to work, dumbfounded.

All day I couldn't stop thinking about that woman. What I really was preoccupied with was deciphering her prayer. What did she mean, *"Don't be anxious about your husband for the Lord will make it clear"*? Did that mean I wasn't going to marry Eli but someone else? Or was I going to marry Eli? Did it at least mean I would get married? I went over it again and again in my head, and once again, I missed the point.

In retrospect, I can imagine that God might have been fed up with my self-obsessed prayers and sent this woman to enlighten me. He told me in the most explicit manner to stop fretting and instead live as a disciple. Live peacefully in this time of waiting. Follow the woman's example. Look beyond myself to my neighbor. Take my eyes off Eli and refocus them on Him. Love Him, and love Him so abundantly that it overflows onto others, just as this woman's love for God had flowed out on me, a stranger.

But I didn't get it. I was so preoccupied with myself and with decoding her words and defining God that I didn't even ask the woman if I could pray for her. I don't even remember her name. And after she left, I didn't even think to spare a prayer for her. It's no wonder I left the church just as confused as when I entered it.

I sacrifice this (I)land unto Thee,
And all whom I loved there, and who loved me;
When I have put our seas 'twixt them and me,
Put thou Thy seas betwixt my sins and Thee.
As the tree's sap doth seek the root below
In winter, in my winter now I go,
Where none but Thee, th' Eternal root
Of true Love, I may know.

—John Donne

There may have been too much of the world in his love. He may have been too attached to the one he lost. Even though we should love our friends, that love shouldn't hinder our love of God, Who must be first.

—Brother Lawrence

Love is not the same thing as desire, for I may desire something without even wishing it well, much less willing its good. I might desire a chocolate ice cream cone, for example. But I do not wish it well; I wish to eat it. This is the difference between lust (mere desire) and love, as between a man and a woman. Desire and love are, of course, compatible when desire is ruled by love; but most people today would, unfortunately, not even know the difference between them. Hence, in our world, love constantly falls prey to lust. That is a major part of the deep sickness of contemporary life.

—Dallas Willard

After the wedding, I slipped outside to look for Eli. He couldn't make it to the ceremony, and I wasn't sure if he knew where the reception was, so I briefly left the side of the bride to find him.

I was in Chicagoland yet again, but this time it wasn't for Eli. It was for my best friend's wedding. Though preoccupied with maid-of-honor responsibilities, I still wanted to see as much of Eli as I could, and I wanted him to meet my college friends. In particular, I hoped the weekend would provide the occasion for a very significant event: a meeting between Eli and my pastor from college.

Let me pause to say a few things about my college pastor. He loves his wife. He loves his babies. And he loves marriage. Like, a lot. As a result, he preached marriage from the pulpit, from behind his espresso machine, and from pretty much anywhere he could. He was a matchmaker aficionado. He was a relational therapist with an MDiv.

According to my pastor, there were only four requirements to look for in a future spouse: That they (1) not be married, (2) not be related, (3) be of the opposite sex, and (4) be a Christian. If he or she met all those requirements, and perhaps as a bonus you were fond of the person, it meant it was time to get hitched.

Naturally, my pastor had always been *very* interested in my love life, and actually he had played quite a large role in my past relationships. And though he had never met Eli, I regularly felt his influence in our relationship. As Eli put it once, my pastor often assumed the role of a Sicilian godfather: not always present, but usually in control. I was eager for my pastor to officially make Eli's acquaintance, but I was also a little afraid.

If my pastor gave his approval, he would immediately start pushing for wedding bells.

At the reception, I lingered close to Eli as the bride and groom were swept off to their honeymoon. I led him around by the hand, introducing him to my friends, all of whom fawned over him. Not only is he an engaging guy, but he looked sharp in his trim black suit and tie.

When all the festivities wrapped up, Eli and I were about to head back into Chicago when I realized my pastor had forgotten to sign the marriage certificate. How perfect. Eli and I drove over to his house. It was the ideal follow-up to the cursory introductions earlier in the day. Immediately my pastor asked us to stay, so we sat around with his wife and kids, laughing and chatting. Then they asked us to stay for dinner. Then coffee.

As we sat around the table, I was beaming. Again, maybe it was just his spiffy tie, but something about Eli gave me great enjoyment that evening. My pastor and his wife were some of the people dearest to my heart, people who knew me well, knew my past and my romantic aspirations. As I saw them connect with Eli, I found myself bragging about him with ease. Under the table, I slid my hand over to his knee and rested it there. In front of these dear people, I felt like Eli was mine, and I was proud of that.

This encouragement was much needed. When I had stood at my best friend's side, watching her commit her life to her husband, my emotions frayed. I was overcome to the point of tears with joy for her. I was also amazed at her ability—any bride's ability, really—to actually walk down the aisle and vow to someone so definitively. The resolve between her and her soon-to-be-husband was remarkable, but it also heightened my own insecurity about marriage in general and Eli in particular. I was discouraged. Things were going wonderfully with Eli, but there was always a hesitancy on my part because, as much as I wanted marriage, I wanted it so much on my own terms that I feared no one, not even Eli, would finally meet me at the altar.

It was an odd paradox. My marriage-happiness was curbed by a fear of commitment. My admiration for Eli was hindered by scrutinizing husband-assessments. I was my own worst enemy, and I definitely wasn't making things easy for Eli. I was hot and cold. I pushed and pulled. I added my own instabilities to the fragility of the relationship. It's amazing we had even made it that far, to the point where I could introduce him to my friends, my pastor. The simple fact that I wanted Eli at the wedding and then found myself basking in his goodness as I led him around gave me hope that maybe this crazy relationship would work after all. I didn't always have resolve, but I had Eli, who continued to pursue my affections and prove that he was perhaps the most worthy admirer I could ever wish for. Maybe he was the one I could pledge myself to. Maybe.

For though it is true enough that men wish to exercise compassion and self-denial and want to have wisdom, etc., yet they wish to determine for themselves the measure, insisting that it shall only be to *a certain degree;* they are not desirous of abolishing all these glorious virtues; on the contrary they would at a good bargain and without inconvenience have the appearance of practicing them. Hence the true divine compassion is unconditionally a sacrifice as soon as it manifests itself in the world.

—Søren Kierkegaard

We had been strolling around Brooklyn Heights all evening, and stopped in a Thai restaurant for dinner. I kept close to Eli, my cold cheek against his arm. We weren't in a rush, but I was feeling impatient, in a hurry to find out where things were headed. As the moon rose overhead, my restlessness increased. I wanted him. I wanted to stop thinking about it.

Eli and I walked another block. "Is that the building?" I asked.

"Not yet, but we're almost there."

I looked up at one of the tallest buildings in downtown Brooklyn. A chill of excitement swept through me. Eli was a good kid, but sometimes too good, too law abiding and conscientious. Tonight, he was going to show me that he wasn't as cautious as I had accused him of being. Tonight, we were going to break into this building and sneak onto the roof.

It may sound silly—you can't fault the heart for a little silliness, right?—but it was important, almost crucial, to know that Eli was adventurous and spontaneous, because I couldn't bear the thought of a calculated life full of careful rules. Shallow as it was, at times his good-boy temperament had been an obstacle to my feelings for him. I was excited to move beyond that ridiculous impediment, and of course to break onto a roof, a favorite pastime of mine.

"Okay, there it is. Do we have a plan?" he asked.

"We should just walk right in and get on the elevator so that we look like we live there," I suggested.

"Sounds good. If I remember correctly, the elevator is on the right."

"And as we pass the doorman, I'm going say something about how I can't believe we forgot to bring our leftovers home."

"Perfect."

I was giddy. I loved this kind of thing. Living in New York without a boyfriend had always felt like a missed opportunity. It is such an enchanting city, but when you have no one to share the romance with, it feels like every little adventure is missing something. But now, with Eli, I was having my romance. I had a partner in crime.

We donned our serious faces, swallowed our laughter, and cruised right in to the building. I almost blew our cover by walking right past the elevator, but within seconds, we were inside and heading up to the thirty-fifth floor.

Impressively—and contrary to my assumptions—Eli had figured out how to get onto the roof the previous summer when he was working in the city. Once out of the elevator, I simply had to follow his lead down the hallway, through a stairwell, and then out a window that Eli opened. He lifted me up, and I shimmied out. I brushed off my knees, pulled my winter hat on tight, and stood up. The view took my breath away.

Manhattan was massive. It shimmered. I felt like I could reach out and touch it. I jumped and skipped with flailing arms. It was exhilarating.

Eli followed me out a few seconds later and shared my astonishment. Breathless, we circled the roof again and again, trying to absorb the city that surrounded us.

In my excitement, I had forgotten the cold, but as soon as we settled against a corner facing the Empire State Building, I began to shiver. Eli gave me his gloves and wrapped his arms around me. I buried my face against him, trying to block the wind.

For those moments, everything was perfect. My restlessness was gone. My youth pulsed through me. My heart was Eli's. I wanted to tell him so, but our words couldn't hold up against the setting. So I held him tighter. I contemplated placing a kiss, our first, on his whiskers. I looked up at him, lingering for a moment, but nothing in his eyes changed. I gazed back out at the city.

Then Eli lowered his face and pressed his lips into mine.

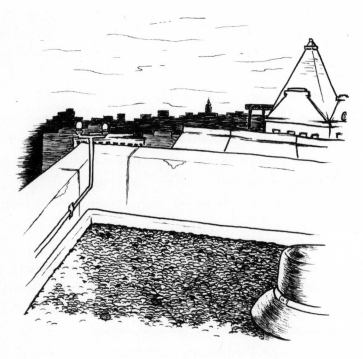

CHAPTER II

BEACH BALLS AND
SEX TALKS

> But the equality of eternity, to will to love one's neighbor,
> seems both too little and too much, and therefore it is as if
> this love to one's neighbor did not fit properly within the
> relationships of earthly existence.
>
> —Søren Kierkegaard

The man on stage moves closer to the microphone.

"See those doors over there?" he asks.

We crane our necks toward the back of the room to see a massive set of double doors swung wide open. We nod our heads.

"Those doors represent the size of the average pore in a condom."

(Silence)

"See this beach ball?"

We nod our heads again.

"This beach ball is your sperm."

(More silence)

"Wanna know what happens when you have 'safe sex'?" The man makes quotation marks with his fingers.

We nod our heads again, tentatively.

The speaker rifles the beach ball through the doors. "*That's* what happens."

And thus began my sex education in the church.

If you know anything about sex ed in the church, you know it's not exactly delicate. *Delicate,* in fact, might be the last word to describe the purity seminars, small groups, and accountability programs I attended in church throughout adolescence. Without a doubt, my youth leaders—often looking nervous—had the best intentions. But even the best intentions, as we all know, aren't always enough.

Our congregations have a tricky job when it comes to adolescents and sex. Not all, but far too many parents are ready to badmouth leaders when things go wrong with their kids, yet largely forget to say thanks when things go right. As I experienced it, my kind-hearted leaders were half guidance counselors—instructing us on how to seek and find the right woman (e.g., "someone who loves the Lord")—and half purity guards shouting, "Keep your pants on!" to the aggressive offenders. The two roles don't always overlap neatly.

Now, throughout my teen years, my youth leaders were there for me in incredibly important ways. I was kept out of loads of trouble I would have found on my own. And when I did find trouble, my youth leaders were generous and reliable friends, ready to counsel me through a range of difficult situations. I can think of one leader in particular (during my junior high years) who was incredibly patient with me. He did more to help me see the truth of Christianity than anyone else prior to college.

But at the same time, the older I get, the more I think there might be some problems with the way we talked about sex in our youth groups. And the way we talked when we were young, naturally influenced the way we thought about marriage later. How we kept (and keep) teenagers out of trouble is often our first entry point for an understanding of marriage.

TUNNEL VISION

If your experience was like mine, your teenage years gave you the impression that sexual behavior was possibly the most important part of being a Christian, or at least one of the most important things.

Case in point: At age fifteen, I had a very specific idea of what my church leaders thought it meant to be pure, yet only a vague understanding of what the Christian life required beyond virginity. Part of this was probably due to my interests at the time, but part of it was a particular focus in my community, a tunnel vision for a certain form of righteousness. This tunnel vision carried with it an unhelpful consequence: Many of my friends and I evaluated commitment to Christ mainly in terms of sexual behavior. As a practical matter, the presence of Christ mainly meant the absence of bad sexual behavior rather than love or the fruit of the Spirit.

This is not to say that one form of obedience should be ignored for another. Sexual immorality is something we must take seriously, the Bible says, and regardless of what our culture says, we should uphold that. And yet a love of God in Christ (and obedience as the manifestation of love) has to be the first foundation of our communities. What good will sexual morality do if we have not love (see 1 Corinthians 13:1–3)?

Now, sexual boundaries are indeed one of the main issues in a teenager's life, and nothing should stop us from trying to keep kids out of trouble. But even these good goals should not obscure the primacy of love and obedience in our communities. And things certainly seem obscured when a teenager's main understanding of fidelity to Christ is sexuality. In other words, if we don't order our topics carefully, the all-encompassing call of Christ (which includes purity) can be replaced with a compartment of good behavior.

I doubt many of us would disagree with any of this in the abstract, but nevertheless, it seems to get lost in the average teen experience—or at least I missed it in mine.

What Happened to Self-Control?

In my youth groups, we loaded marriage up with huge expectations. Marriage was often presented as the sole remedy for lust, and therefore, great hopes of sexual satisfaction were attached to it. As I understood it in my teenage years, it was marriage, not a life given to God, that was the remedy for sexual desires I couldn't fulfill. I merely had to control desire until marriage, then I was home free.

Of course, the Bible *does* prescribe marriage this way (recall "it is better to marry than to burn with passion" in 1 Corinthians 7:9), but it's *not the only* biblical solution. Another one is self-denial, which is a significant part of discipleship. As we've discussed, self-denial, or living without something we want, can be a valuable practice, and to deny ourselves out of obedience or in response to grace can begin to transform our desires. The Bible also recommends self-control, a fruit of the Spirit, as something that will naturally flow out of a transformed follower of Christ (see 1 Corinthians 7:8–9, 37–38; Galatians 5:23). Certainly, then, both self-control and self-denial are biblical visions of how we might avoid sexual sin. And yet in my experience, I heard only about marriage when it came to sex.

If this is a message you heard—marriage is the main fix for lust—I think it can create possible problems for couples down the road.

The first is that marriage doesn't solve all our lust problems. "True love waits" naturally implies a finish line, either for love, sex, or both. The phrase hints that our wait will, at some point, stop. And yet, as many of us know, the waiting does not stop, and love, to the contrary, is something to be nurtured and grown into rather than acquired in a moment.

This is true both physically and relationally, and also as it relates to our sin. The fact that the married life is not free of lust and struggle might seem obvious to anyone with a few married friends, and yet we don't have to search long before we hear someone speak as if marriage ends the battle. Teen purity talks more than implied this idea that marriage was the great solution to sexual sin—or at least they did for me.

Second, if marriage was presented as the main fix for lust, perhaps it was because we often had only a shallow vision of self-denial. If self-denial or self-control to us meant only that we didn't have sex until we got married, and *then* we could gratify ourselves, we missed one of the larger implications of discipleship and of following Christ. Discipleship is not just hanging on until marriage; it is, as we've said, a gradual and complete reordering of all our desires, sexual and otherwise, so that we can live more wholly for Christ.

Learning to say no to our desires is a major part of orienting our lives toward God, and it can often be a life-giving discipline. It might not always be practical for hormonal teens, but it's possible that things could look different if teens seek purity out of a desire to give their lives to Christ, rather than just to "save themselves" for a spouse. The two goals may overlap in quite a few circumstances, but in others, they are undoubtedly different.

Indeed, if we said, "Deny yourself" instead of "True love waits," and if we practice setting aside desires rather than just hanging on until we can satisfy them, we might be less surprised and better prepared for the actual challenges of marriage. We might be ready for the wide range of sacrifices marriage requires. A better-rehearsed practice of self-denial and self-control would almost certainly train us to bring more grace and self-lessness into all that we do, including marriage.

Furthermore, if self-denial were to be emphasized in our adolescent sex seminars, rather than only marriage-as-carrot, singles might also find themselves better prepared for navigating the challenge of purity as a single adult. There would, most likely, be fewer discouraged singles who give in. And there would be fewer singles who succumb to temptation because they think, *"What's the harm? No point in holding out if there isn't true love waiting for me."* If we frame purity in terms of discipleship and not marriage, singleness would lose some of its dread and instead be valued as a fruitful position for learning Christlikeness. Rather than feeling frustrated in a holding pattern, anyone who is single might more readily see the value and particular grace of his or her situation.

TRUE LOVE WAITS—AND IS DISAPPOINTED

In attempts to rein in teenage sexuality, my communities more or less tended to stretch the truth about married sex. One of the worst of these well-intentioned almost-truths is what I'll call "reward sex"—the term is mine—and I think the idea might be somewhat common.

The story went like this: If you behaved well and didn't have sex before marriage, God would reward you with extra-awesome-and-uncomplicated sex once you made it to the wedding night. If you saved yourself until the honeymoon, God paid you back with a super amazing first night. In other words, expectations for sex in marriage are spruced up to try to nudge teenage hopes in the right direction.

Without doubt, this was done with the best intentions. But as a theological matter and a matter of reasonable reality, it seems a little unhelpful. The fact is, even if true love waits, it is often disappointed.

I may not earn admiration from anyone, parents in particular, for pointing this out. Some people might even say I'm encouraging the wrong type of behavior. I'm not. The point here is that if a stretched truth is the only thing securing our obedience, I'm not sure I'm comfortable with the type of obedience we've secured.

By ensuring good behavior from unmarried people with promises of "reward sex," we have, I think, missed an important piece of what the Christian life is about. We don't obey because obedience is currency that brings us our desire tenfold down the road. We obey because Jesus told us to. We shouldn't obey out of a calculated exchange for future earthly reward—we should obey out of love.

It's true that following Christ has its rewards in heaven, and on earth there are great blessings that flow from loving God first. However, those blessings are usually not our wishes granted exponentially, but rather God's leading us toward what He knows is best. The blessing of obedience is not automatically awesome marital sex but a life lived with God. Purity is undoubtedly a worthy aim, but maybe we don't need to strain the reality of marriage so much to achieve it.

Eli struck another match. The wind blew it out. He tried another. I cupped my hand around the end of the cigar and turned my back to the lake. As Eli held the flame close to my face, I inhaled, deeply.

My cigar finally lit. He lit his. Soon they both went out again.

The night was frigid, antagonizing not only our cigars but also our bones. The wind grazed our palms, chilling our bodies. Smoke warmed our lungs and capillaries, and it distracted us from the nonsense of the barren Lake Michigan bank, both of us struggling to make a dent in the winter cold. But neither of us disputed the perfection of our decision.

We had finished dinner hours before—a deliberately romantic dinner since it was Valentine's Day. But eating a nice dinner at a nice restaurant while sitting in nice clothes was not really my thing, nor Eli's, so the evening really began when we walked to the closest corner store and bought the cheapest pack of cigars they sold: $4.99 for a pack of two.

I was clinging to his arm as we hurried down the sidewalk to the beach, cigars in his coat pocket. Our words shook in our mouths.

"I am more afraid of you because of what I read," Eli said. "It might be a silly thing to say, but I mean it in the very best way."

He was referring to a poem I had written and sent him a few days before. His comment shook me. A high compliment from a man who, I was learning, had a vast interior, who only praised something he truly admired. The idea of my writing connecting with him in such a way was beautiful. It chilled me.

At the lakefront, we stood, then sat, then stood, unable to decide which was warmer. The beach was dull and frozen, neither illuminated by light nor consumed by darkness. Some stray streetlights and harbor lamps brightened the shore. I was hoping for total darkness; I wanted to look out into the water and see nothing. A steep specification, since we were in the middle of Chicago.

He again lit my cigar, which was now longer than his. As the match came between his face and mine, Eli's eyes cleared. Green. Intent. I looked down. I forgot to breathe in this time. He took out another match.

His cigar burned down more quickly than mine. He was able to keep his lit, even against the wind, while I forgot to tend to my kindling. I took too much enjoyment from flicking off the ashes. I was content with the aroma that his cigar created and forgot to keep my own guarded from the lake's gusts. And I might have been talking too much—I can't remember. In my memory, the evening was quiet and still.

I wondered about the smell that clutched my coat. Would it ever come out? I was thinking about Eli. Why didn't he stand closer to me? I wanted us to talk more, to discuss whatever it is they say can't be spoken for its fragility and dimness. But our teeth were chattering, catching our words. We were both growing lightheaded.

Finally, my cigar was gone too.

"Good night," I said, holding back tears. I hung up the phone. It was 1 a.m. and I was alone in the dark at my kitchen table. I sat dumbfounded for a moment, fiddling with the tablecloth. Then I started crying. Eli and I had just broken up.

Neither of us had planned it—at least not consciously, I think—but after our phone conversation, it was clear we had both been having misgivings. We were hitting a point where logistics could no longer be ignored. Eli had plans to move to San Francisco, where he had a good job lined up, and I was in book publishing, an industry exclusive to New York. In the foreseeable future, neither of us could imagine moving for the sake of the other. We both felt drawn to opposite coasts, and a move from the places where we belonged was too much, too soon. Things were going well, but neither of us could justify the upheaval required by leaving our respective cities. We saw the potential, but the potential wasn't enough at that point in time, which was hard to face. Airfare was adding up. Vacation days were depleted. And the emotional distance was taking its toll.

So we broke up, and this is how it went down.

A week earlier, Eli had expressed a few concerns and asked for some space to think things through. He was at a crossroads that was forcing him to nail down his plans for the upcoming year, and with me in the picture, everything was a lot more complicated. I was a little concerned, but I also welcomed the time it gave me to think through the trajectory of our relationship. Where could this possibly go?

Eli called me that night while I was out at a reading. I got home late but gave him a ring once I was back in my apartment. We shot the breeze for a while. Then Eli began explaining to me where he had been mentally and emotionally that week. He was still struggling to figure things out and hadn't found the clarity he had hoped for. I likewise had been feeling uneasy for reasons I couldn't put my finger on, and during that week I had lost some confidence that I might have a future with Eli. The bottom line was that neither of us was more committed to each other than to our current situations, and we weren't willing to uproot and relocate, which seemed to be the only way the relationship could continue.

We talked through these issues, trying to find a compromise and speaking openly about our concerns. But in the end, the result was something neither of us wanted. We agreed to call it off. It made sense. It was civil, mutual. But that didn't make it easier.

I sat in my kitchen for a while after the call. I wasn't tired and didn't want to wake up my roommates. I wiped the tears from my eyes, made some tea, and prepared for a meeting I had the next day.

I was heartbroken.

I had been home in California for spring break when we broke up, and the phone call changed everything about the week. It sounds cliché, but I honestly remember only vague details about the days that followed: wandering around my parents' house, writing songs that felt lifeless, drafting e-mails and deleting them, normal activities sagging under sadness. I went to a friend's house but couldn't even tell him what had happened.

I remember the looks on my parents' faces as we sat around at the kitchen table that night. Both of them were surprised, but my Mom looked particularly sad. She loved Claire and couldn't understand why we'd called it off. I felt as if I wanted to reverse our decision just to undo the expression on her face.

I tried to explain: On one hand, the conversation with Claire hadn't been a total surprise. Like Claire said, we had struggled to know what our careers and commitments meant to where we'd live, and our plans were forcing us to make decisions that were too heavy for our young relationship. Things were going well, but it was all still *so new.* The distance between New York and San Francisco was pushing us to know the future before the future could be known, and neither of us knew what to do with that. We were on different sides of the country, and neither of us was ready for a commitment that would draw us beyond that.

On the other hand, there was much to be surprised about. Our conversation had gone peacefully, yet the emotions that surged up afterward were anything but. I had barely hung up the phone before I was stricken by a swelling *what just happened?*—a wave of pulsing unease that washed over me completely. It was confusing. I couldn't make sense of how I felt.

And so I lingered in that confusion for some time: doubt, queasiness, second-guessing. It was like the decision made sense somewhere in my mind, but I couldn't *feel* the logic. I was floating. We had chosen to move ahead, but once the motion began, it all felt too soon and irrevocable. Had we made the right choice? Did we know what we had done? Had our whole relationship been a waste?

The distance between us was suddenly greater than ever before. We exchanged a terse e-mail a few days later, then all communication stopped. The stillness crept in. Gone were the playful e-mails and daily calls, and a void of silence opened where the relationship had been.

As in the T. S. Eliot poem, it ended not with a bang but a whimper.

CHAPTER 12

LONELINESS, THE ACHE

But the more I think about loneliness, the more I think that
the wound of loneliness is like the Grand Canyon—a deep
incision in the surface of our existence which has become
an inexhaustible source of beauty and self-understanding.

—Henri J. M. Nouwen

Loneliness is many things to many people. It differs widely person to
person, and yet we all know the sensation when we feel it. For some, it's
the fear of being alone in the future. For others, it's the feeling of being
alone in the moment. For others still, it's the disappointment we suffer in
the presence of another. For me, it's often a little of each, though one or
another becomes dominant at any given moment. But whatever form it
takes, nearly all of us have felt the gnaw. And amidst all the varieties of
our loneliness, one thing is constant: no one likes to be alone, and almost
all of us avoid it if we can.

Three days after I hung up the phone with Eli—a small act that
clinched a big decision—it hit me. I was enjoying homemade huevos
rancheros for breakfast in our kitchen with my roommate and some out-
of-town friends when Eli came up in the conversation.

"How are things with you and Eli?" my friend asked cheerfully.

I turned red. I tried to stab a few black beans with my fork and acted like I had taken a large bite that required an unusual amount of time to swallow. Then after wiping my mouth with my napkin, I muttered, "Oh, we broke up."

My roommate immediately jumped in, upset that I hadn't told her sooner. And then the questions came. But just as quickly, I pushed the questions away, assuring them it was all fine, it was all mutual, it was all for the better, and so there really wasn't much to discuss. Begrudgingly, they changed the subject.

But it was too late. The gaping hole Eli had left in my life had been poked, and I could no longer deny it was there…and it hurt.

Shades of Loneliness

One of the first things loneliness corrodes is self-confidence. Loneliness is the deep inward suspicion in our hearts that we are not cool enough, not interesting enough, or not smart, attractive, or successful enough to be worth the love and attention of others. For example, even though Eli and I had mutually agreed to end things between us, I soon felt an irrational offense from the breakup. Why hadn't we wanted to fight for the relationship? Why hadn't we tried to persuade each other? I felt deficient. If I had been smarter, prettier, or more irresistible in some way, he wouldn't have let me go so easily. I must have been a disappointment to him. And as my self-esteem deflated, a gloomy feeling of isolation swelled.

Times of loneliness can vary in length, and mine certainly did. For some people, loneliness is a constant, a stable and powerful sorrow that cannot be shaken no matter how vigorous the effort. For me, it was more fickle. It came and went in degrees. Sometimes I wallowed in it, and other times I denied it. But one thing I couldn't shake was the thought that loneliness might be my future. The event had magnified not only my momentary loneliness, but also the possibility of long-term loneliness, because when I cut out the possibility that I would marry Eli, things looked pretty dismal. Eli and I had been so good for each other! We were so compatible! He was pretty much everything I thought I wanted. So if it wasn't Eli, I concluded that it probably wasn't anybody. If I couldn't make myself fall madly in love with a catch as good as Eli, then I was simply incapable of that sort of connection and wasn't meant to fall in love. Feeling not only unlovable but also unable to love is a pretty lonely place to be.

Loneliness can be a powerful motivation behind the actions and events of our lives, whatever they may be. In my own case, I turned to work. I thought my job and the identity it provided would be the thing to dull the ache and provide meaning for my increasingly certain future as a spinster. I reasoned that I might as well fortify the career so I'd at least have something when I was old and alone.

The fear of loneliness can drive us not only to restless busyness regarding work but also to excessive long-term planning, to immediate and endless wanderings, or even toward hyper-socializing. Loneliness can nudge us not only toward ambitious careers but also to "good" activities in our churches and communities. And it can do the opposite as well: It can drive us into a state of inertia, resulting in a lethargic apathy that weighs us down so heavily all our tasks feel burdensome and undirected. It can make life look so dismal that we withdraw from our responsibilities and relationships.

THE LASTING ACHE

Loneliness can also drive us into the arms of others. It isn't the only reason we seek relationships, to be sure, but it certainly can be a major one. As God said in Genesis, there's something deep and instinctual about the fact that it's not good for man or a woman to be alone (see Genesis 2:18). We know it in our bones.

Even though I was trying to get used to the idea of singleness all over again, my heart was still hopeful that there was another pair of arms out there to embrace me and not let me go. But the truth is, even if there *was* such a love, deep down I knew that my loneliness wouldn't go away. Even if love is sleeping beside us, loneliness can remain. Contrary to what we want to believe, it doesn't find its complete antidote in marriage, nor in any relationship for that matter. "If you get married…[and end up] putting the weight of all your deepest hopes and longings on the person you are marrying," Tim Keller writes, "you are going to crush him or her with your expectations. It will distort your life and your spouse's life in a hundred ways. No person, not even the best one, can give your soul all it needs."[1] And likewise, Henri Nouwen observes, "Many marriages are ruined because neither partner was able to fulfill the often hidden hope that the other would take his or her loneliness away."[2]

Because loneliness is uncomfortable, even agonizing, it is simply our nature to place our hopes in some future other—a boyfriend, a spouse, a child—and we expect that they will provide companionship, intimacy, or meaning that will stave off our feelings of isolation. We channel loneliness into the search for a person and conclude that we must and should find that other precisely because the feeling is so strong.

Relationships certainly do provide profound meaning in our lives. To have a dear friend, a spouse, a child, is to have a relationship that is incredibly significant, and these relationships animate and bring beauty to many other parts of our lives. They can make us feel intensely loved and consequential. But the thing is this—and this is what we can sometimes forget: loneliness sticks. Regardless of how our films, books, or poems romanticize the idea that a relationship will meet our deepest needs, loneliness is a fixed reminder that we remain incomplete. Even the worthiest, most glorious relationship will not satisfy our deepest needs.

If loneliness exists regardless of our relational status, then I wonder if maybe there is more to it than we typically consider. If loneliness sticks, maybe there is a reason. And just maybe, if we can grasp that reason, loneliness doesn't have to be the anathema our hearts, our friends, and our society say it is. Maybe we shouldn't run from loneliness so quickly, but instead turn our eyes toward it and ask what its presence in our lives might mean.

A Gift

Perhaps the best place to start is with Henri Nouwen's reflection:

> But the more I think about loneliness, the more I think that the wound of loneliness is like the Grand Canyon—a deep incision in the surface of our existence which has become an inexhaustible source of beauty and self-understanding.
>
> Therefore I would like to voice loudly and clearly what might seem unpopular and maybe even disturbing: The Christian way of life does not take away our loneliness; it protects it and cherishes it as a precious gift. Sometimes it seems as if we do everything possible to avoid the painful confrontation with our basic human loneliness, and allow ourselves to be trapped by false gods promising immediate satisfaction and quick relief. But perhaps the painful awareness of loneliness is an invitation to transcend our limitations and look beyond the boundaries of our existence. The awareness of our loneliness might be a gift we must protect and guard, because our loneliness reveals to us an inner emptiness that can be destructive when misunderstood, but filled with promise for him who can tolerate its sweet pain.

When we are impatient, when we want to give up our loneliness and try to overcome the separation and incompleteness we feel, too soon, we easily relate to our human world with devastating expectations. We ignore what we already know with a deepseated, intuitive knowledge—that no love or friendship, no intimate embrace or tender kiss, no community, commune or collective, no man or woman, will ever be able to satisfy our desire to be released from our lonely condition. This truth is so disconcerting and painful that we are more prone to play games with our fantasies than to face the truth of our existence. Thus we keep hoping that one day we will find the man who really understands our experiences, the woman who will bring peace to our restless life, the job where we can fulfill our potentials, the book which will explain everything, and the place where we can feel at home. Such false hope leads us to make exhausting demands and prepares us for bitterness and dangerous hostility when we start discovering that nobody, and nothing, can live up to our absolutistic expectations.[3]

If we took time to examine our loneliness—standing still for a moment, instead of running after activity or recoiling in apathy—perhaps we could see how our loneliness isn't something to automatically avoid. We might discover its transcendence, meaning we might see how it can carry us through our own worries and gloom and bring us closer to God. This doesn't mean that the gnawing goes away, but that the gnawing can be a reminder of what is good, just as a cut on our finger makes us all the more aware of the importance of that finger, or just as a broken window makes us appreciate the warmth of a home. Indeed, sometimes it takes the lack of something to reveal what we actually value. Consider what Marilynne Robinson writes in her novel, *Housekeeping:*

For need can blossom into all the compensation it requires. To crave and to have are as like a thing and its shadow. For when does a berry break upon the tongue as sweetly as when one longs to taste it, and when is the taste refracted into so many hues and savors of ripeness and earth, and when do our senses know any thing so utterly as when we lack it?[4]

When do we know our need for communion with a complete being more than when we lack it? When does God's presence feel more divine than when our senses have longed unsuccessfully for Him, and then He bursts upon our taste buds in all His fullness? "Oh, taste and see that the LORD is good! Blessed is the man who takes refuge in him!" the psalmist sings (Psalm 34:8). But how often do we sear our taste buds by sampling too many pleasures and dim our sight by staring at too many artificial lights? How often do we seek refuge from our loneliness in the things of this world, even seemingly good human relationships, instead of in the Lord?

Our loneliness can point to the fulfillment that God alone provides, but only if we direct our cravings toward Him. We must learn to identify our need for *Him* in the thick of our ache. We must begin to know a response to loneliness that isn't a reflexive desire for anyone or anything but God. In this way, loneliness doesn't always have to be a constant source of weariness that turns in on itself, but a source that has a purpose outside itself, which is to draw our weary souls to the Lord who will renew us (see Isaiah 40:31).

And just as soon as we are renewed, we will again beg for His rejuvenation. Just as soon as He breaks sweetly upon our taste buds, our tongues will long for Him with a new vigor. The stunning truth in our God-given appetites is that even as we are filled to overflowing, we still hunger and thirst. "O God, I have tasted Thy goodness, and it has both satisfied me and made me thirsty for more,"[5] A. W. Tozer prayed.

Loneliness reveals our desires with stinging clarity; it can wrench open our hearts wide to God if we let it. When we feel inadequate—unattractive, uncool, unsuccessful—His grace is available if we are willing to receive it. When we lose our pride, new room is created for God to enter and become our boasting. When we lose our certainty of what lies ahead, we have an opportunity to relinquish control and follow Christ into the unknown.

These things won't always happen automatically. We must be still enough to peer into our loneliness if it is ever to lead us back to Him. If we run to other hopes too quickly, or if we run to created things rather than to the Creator, we risk failing to acknowledge the true depth of our need for God. If we seek out human relationships before we seek God, we might in fact become devastated by our own loneliness.

In the worst-case scenario, our longing means we walk into church and scan the pews for the handsome guy without a ring on his finger or the cute girl sitting alone. It makes us so self-oriented that we walk into church looking *for love instead of the One who can teach us how to love.* Or because of our loneliness, we involve ourselves in the activities of our churches, looking for the respect we are missing in our relationships. Loneliness can energize even seemingly noble activities with insincere motivations. We also might abandon community altogether in order to mope in our dejection. Loneliness drives us away from others and into ourselves, where we surely will find no respite. In either instance, if we are honest in our hearts, loneliness becomes a spiritual impediment instead of a wellspring.

But it doesn't need to be that way if we have the patience to be still. Loneliness sticks, but it need not devour. Loneliness can instead be the quiet current that over and over again turns our hearts to God, bringing us to the feet of His Son who loves us more deeply, more significantly, and more abundantly than anyone we will find in this life.

When God at first made man,
Having a glass of blessings standing by;
"Let us," said he, "pour on him all we can:
Let the world's riches, which dispersed lie,
Contract into a span."

So strength first made a way;
Then beauty flowed, then wisdom, honour, pleasure.
When almost all was out, God made a stay,
Perceiving that alone, of all his treasure,
Rest in the bottom lay.

"For if I should," said he,
"Bestow this jewel also on my creature,
He would adore my gifts instead of me,
And rest in Nature, not the God of Nature:
So both should losers be.

"Yet let him keep the rest,
But keep them with repining restlessness;
Let him be rich and weary, that at least,
If goodness lead him not, yet weariness
May toss him to my breast."

     —George Herbert, "The Pulley"

Description of man: dependence, desire [for] independence, needs.

     —Blaise Pascal

Since my first correspondence with Claire, I had been excited about the possibility of Us. I had seen a great deal that was incredible about Claire, and even when I only knew the vague outline of who she was, I thought she was remarkable. Her mind, her heart, her person; she was a bright reminder of God's limitless creativity.

Then we paraded around the country, getting to know each other more deeply weekend after weekend, sitting on rooftops, watching movies, discussing books, and strolling through our cities. It wasn't long before I started to edge closer to the sense that marriage might be right around the bend for me.

Claire brought out a lot in me, but perhaps what was most surprising was how our relationship stirred up questions I had never asked so deeply before. Just as soon as our romance grew toward real expectation, it collapsed, and I couldn't help but ask what I had been aiming for in all that had happened.

Certainly the romance had been a compelling experience on its own, but I knew enough from married friends to know that the initial thrill might not always stay. What motivations of mine would remain if and when the feeling sputtered? I tried to be as honest as possible with myself.

I knew I wanted to be loved. I wanted a teammate. I wanted beauty up close. I wanted companionship. I wanted a building block for a family. I wanted sex.

In the back of my mind, there was a notion of needing to form a "Christian marriage" or a "Christian family," together with a vague sense of what it possibly meant to be a Christian man. I also didn't want to be left out. Many of my friends were either married or soon to be married, and I was hardly excited by the idea of being the lone single at couples' nights—or not invited at all.

I also felt apprehension about being the unmarried thirty-something at church, the brother in Christ I'd seen families glance at with suspicion. I knew no pastor or elder who was single, and I was aware of few single adults active in congregational leadership.

As I began to see how Claire could provide the future I wanted—and how she could steer me away from the one I didn't want—I naturally started to pursue her more seriously. If I had indeed found the girl who would put all these pieces together, I would be a fool not to put a ring on her finger, right?

So when I took the step of asking her to be my girlfriend, I saw a field of exciting possibilities open up. Good things. I saw us writing music together. I saw us sitting up late talking about Marilynne Robinson. I saw us traveling through Europe, India, and Asia. I saw us watching films, sharing stories, becoming better stewards of our creative abilities. In Claire I saw the opportunity for experiences I might not otherwise enjoy. And I wanted them.

What I did not consider, however, as obvious as it is now, was what God might have been asking of me or what might have been best for Claire. In the hurry of working toward the vision of life I saw ahead, I didn't find much concern in my heart for God or for Claire, my neighbor. Instead, as long as things continued to move forward, I assumed that Claire's mere presence in my life and my continued attraction to that presence was enough. I saw no flaws in that. And no one challenged me to seek a broader vision.

Claire was what I wanted, and as I had heard from almost every philosophical input in my life—family, church, friends, society— choosing a spouse meant *matching what you wanted with what the other person had*. You might not get everything, of course, and you should be

prepared to live with disappointment—no relationship was perfect—
but the starting point was clear: Track down the person *who best fits what
you want.* (And, as an afterthought, hope you meet the requirements of
your spouse.)

And so I did what I was supposed to do: I evaluated her as thoroughly as I could, considering what she had in relation to what I wanted.
I didn't always think of the situation in such cold and sterile terms, but
that was what was happening.

As I pieced this together later, I was less than inspired by how the
process went. And troubled. If other Christians went about things the
way I did, what were our spouse searches beyond the largest and longest
purchasing event in our lives? I knew marriage could spark great spiritual
growth, but what did a distinctly *Christian pursuit* of marriage mean beyond a no-return policy, poorly observed?

The problem wasn't that I took delight in Claire, for certainly God
had been generous in allowing us to meet and grow together. No, the
problem was that the search had revolved around me. Claire, in one sense,
had become a means by which I could assemble the life I wanted.

But Claire was more than a means.

I hadn't known the difference then, but in a hundred ways, Claire
was more than merely what I wanted, more than a set of expectations.

And it hadn't just been with Claire. I had spent years of my young
adult life refining my ability to scrutinize others, much of it in the name
of seeking marriage. My search was hardly charitable, and my past relationships attested to it. I was perpetually *expecting more,* grasping for
something more even as I myself knew I would never completely satisfy
someone else. Past relationships had been a "chance to grow," where so-
called growth meant demanding more, and scrutinizing the next person
even more carefully. In some instances, "growth" meant learning generosity, but that was the exception. Relational wisdom tended to accumu-

late by way of elimination; the thing I learned from past relationships was what wouldn't work for me. And in that sense, I had indeed "grown." After a series of relationships, I had a far more specific sense of what I wanted, or what would "work" for me. Like a shopper, I knew what distinguished the items on the shelves. And unless something changed, I would stroll the aisles until I found the right item, or until I no longer had the will to shop. And I believed this all was to my benefit.

Looking back, this makes me queasy.

Looking back, I wonder how my life might have looked if I had learned to see others the way Christ did, if I had made His love my object rather than finding The One.

The more I learn about Him, the less I think Jesus is all that interested in meeting my lengthy list of criteria, a list that grows and shifts by the day and is rarely consistent even with itself.

"What benefit is it to you if you love only those who love you in return?"

No, I think He wants us to humble ourselves. I think He wants us to look not only to our own interests, but also to the interests of others.

I think He wants to inflame His love within us.

I had gotten it all wrong with Claire.

Months after we had broken up, Eli and I met up at my church, the first time we had seen each other since ending things. The smell of his freshly showered hair was distracting. Standing close to him, singing from the hymnal he held in front of us, I struggled to follow the verses. My mind was racing. *"Why had we broken up?"* I asked myself.

When I first heard Eli would be in town visiting friends, I really hoped I would get to see him. I just thought it would be nice to catch up. I had no idea his mere presence next to me would be so overwhelming.

My surprise was not unfounded. In the ensuing months after we had broken things off, we were all too successful at parting ways. Eli had finished up law school in Chicago and began forging a new life. I was still trying to keep my head above water in New York. We kept our distance and created a new sense of equilibrium apart from each other. We e-mailed here and there but for the most part moved forward with our separate lives.

Until, unexpectedly, a friendship started to emerge. Somehow, after we each found some footing, our occasional e-mails became just a little more frequent. But I was still skeptical. As much as I thought it would be nice to stay friends with Eli, I knew how rare it was for a romantic relationship to settle peacefully into a friendship, particularly a substantial one. I myself had had past relationships that didn't end so well, so I didn't have high hopes that Eli and I would be able to make the transition. When I hung up the phone after that conclusive call, I had decided the less we heard from each other the better, which Eli can attest to from my many curt replies to his periodic e-mails.

But things ended up differently with Eli. When time began to clear the confusion, we remembered the promises we made in that little café when we first started dating. Out of grace, we were given a mutual desire to appreciate one another above and beyond our initial hopes. A new experience grew in us, one that was rich with a new kind of potential. At times it was more natural than others, but we were determined to see it through.

The outcome of our efforts was lovely indeed. Though our interactions were still just little taps across long distances, they rang a sweet note. I remember one conversation in which we discussed a favorite book. With the phone to my ear, as I lay across my bed, we laughed and bantered like we had done many times before. Eli and I were finally at ease again.

Not long after that, Eli scheduled a trip to New York. He was coming to visit friends. He had deferred his job one year and was using his time to travel and touch base with several buds who were scattered across the States, some of whom had invited him to New York. His trip had nothing to do with me, and so while I knew I no longer had any particular claim on him, I was hoping for at least a little of his attention while he was in town.

"Don't be a stranger!" I wrote when he told me he would be back in Brooklyn.

I blocked off much of the week, not knowing exactly when he would be free to hang. I went about my days, hoping to hear from him, but it wasn't until church on Sunday morning that we finally met.

When I slid into the seat next to him, I felt comfortable. But I was also thrown off. I hadn't expected him to look so handsome. My eagerness to see Eli had had everything to do with clearing the air, cementing our routine as friends, and just enjoying time with a good pal. I was relieved that things felt normal and right between us. But also perplexed. Things felt a little too normal and right between us. So much so that I wondered what had ever gone wrong. Part of me wanted to wrap my arm around his waist as we sang. It felt unnatural not to.

It was a gray Sunday. As we walked out from the service, ominous clouds plastered the sky. We risked the chance of rain to grab greasy empanadas and walk again through Central Park. Wandering underneath the bare trees, we found the park was eerily empty. It provided just enough space for Eli and me to adjust. This visit to the park was indeed different from our first stroll. It was more full, more textured, like the cloudy sky.

We found a bench to sit on where we talked and picked at our lunch. There was a quiet urgency to our conversation. It was surprising what we didn't know about each other's lives, but also surprising how easily we connected as if no time had passed. There we remained for much of the afternoon.

Then midsentence I looked at my watch. I was late to a friend's baby shower. Eli walked me to my subway stop, and we waved good-bye.

CHAPTER 13

SOLITUDE, THE POSTURE

But when you pray, go into your room and shut the door
and pray to your Father who is in secret. And your Father
who sees in secret will reward you.

—Matthew 6:6

Be still, and know that I am God.

—Psalm 46:10

Being alone isn't only about loneliness, of course. It can also be about solitude.

While loneliness reminds us that we long for God, solitude is the productive quiet in which we seek Him. Loneliness is a signpost, while solitude can be a garden. That is, loneliness is often a feeling of estrangement that has the potential to point us to God. Solitude, on the other hand, is seclusion that can provide a context for reflection, meditation, and growth. It is the halting of our frenzied lives for the purpose of seeking God, listening, prayer, and a movement toward knowing Him more deeply in the whole of who we are. It is a halting of whatever is clamoring for our attention at the moment.

I've recently wondered if some of our marriage-happiness keeps us

loneliness vs. solitude

from this, from seeing the spiritual usefulness of solitude. In the hurry to form and maintain our relationships, I wonder if we sometimes forget how we form on our own before God.

As I thought about this, I was reminded of some lines in a poem about marriage a friend showed me. "Give your hearts, but not into each other's keeping," the poem went. "For only the hand of Life can contain your hearts." And then a few lines later: "And the oak tree and the cypress grow not in each other's shadow."[1]

The poet's point is that even though we grow close to one another in marriage, we should also remember that we grow primarily in God. An oak tree doesn't grow because of the cypress tree nearby, but because of the sun. So it is with our lives before God.

Admittedly, this poem is hardly authority, but in one way, you might think of it as a variation of Paul's point in 1 Corinthians 7. As we've discussed, rather than lifting up marriage's potential to sanctify, Paul highlights the potential of marriage to divide our attention. The description feels odd because of how we're used to talking about marriage: We more often think of marriage as a gift or growth stimulant than as binding us to someone who could block out God's light from our lives. We emphasize Ephesians 5:22–33—husbands are to love their wives as Christ loves the church—over 1 Corinthians 7. We spotlight sanctification, but say less about idolatry. Instead, I think we could probably hold both in better biblical tension.

In a society reeling from broken families and divorce, it's natural to see why our emphasis would lean toward Ephesians 5 over 1 Corinthians 7. If marriages break down now more than ever, a sacrificial love by husbands for their wives is great advice for a host of people.

And yet the cost of leaning too heavily on Ephesians 5 is that we underemphasize the importance of growing before God on our own; we downplay marriage's ability to impede our vertical relationship.

We don't need to choose one or the other—marriage or solitude. It's not either/or, but both/and. Just as Bonhoeffer wrote in *Life Together*, "Let him who cannot be alone beware of community.... Let him who is not in community beware of being alone.... Each by itself has profound pitfalls and perils."[2] We should grow both in solitude *and* in our horizontal relationships.

BE STILL

If we suffer from an extreme, however, I don't think it's an overemphasis on solitude. Pascal wrote, "All the unhappiness of men arises from one single fact, that they cannot stay quietly in their own chamber,"[3] and I think he's right, now more than ever. Being alone is something we frantically avoid, and we recoil deeply from opportunities to *be still, and know that [He is] God*, as the psalmist said.

As evidence for this, consider the way I responded after Claire and I broke up. Once I didn't have a girlfriend in my life, I suddenly had lots of extra time. The time I would have spent writing Claire, talking on the phone, or making trips to and from New York was again mine. And what did I do with my time? I dove deeply into *activity*, mainly school and music. At times, I loved my new freedom and flexibility. At other times, I felt a sense of loss, and my activities felt like sad attempts at escapism. In hindsight, I *wish* I would have used that season to learn how to be still, instead of bustling around to avoid how I felt.

Solitude is certainly not just for post-breakup periods, but in my case, the breakup between Claire and me could have been a starting point for a better understanding of stillness—the act of just being and listening. Rather than running from the way I felt, I could have seen it as a chance to grow.

Most of us don't like solitude, and I certainly didn't. Perhaps we don't mind the *idea* of it, but we rarely do it. We turn on the TV, check the web, or e-mail a friend. We do anything we can to keep up the steady stream of activity, because when activities cease, things don't always feel right. As Henri Nouwen described it, "As soon as we are alone...an inner chaos opens up in us,"[4] and that scares many of us. We find importance and identity in busyness, and we cling to it.

Put another way, solitude "is to choose to do nothing. For extensive periods of time. All accomplishment is given up.... It is enough that God is God and we are his."[5] Or as Thomas Merton described it, in solitude we cultivate an " 'attitude,' an 'outlook': faith, openness, attention, reverence, expectation, supplication, trust, joy. All these finally permeate our being with love in so far as our living faith tells us we are in the presence of God [and] that we live in Christ."[6]

SCULPTED IN SOLITUDE

Solitude can be a powerful force in our lives in at least a couple ways. First, in the clamor of our busyness, and in the midst of busy congregational lives, solitude can add vitality to prayer. Remember what Jesus said in the Sermon on the Mount: "But when you pray, go into your room and shut the door and pray to your Father who is in secret. And your Father who sees in secret will reward you" (Matthew 6:6). Praying in solitude is prayer that is generally more honest, a prayer separated from our desire to be known and seen.

Second, solitude helps with the process of true inward change. For all the usefulness and beauty of self-denial, there can be danger too. If you grit your teeth and change only external behavior, you risk being like the Pharisees who cleaned only the outside of their cup. The Pharisees projected righteousness to others while their insides, according to Jesus, remained full of "greed and self-indulgence" (Matthew 23:25).

For the love of God to truly take root, our transformation must be inward first, then outward. God must pervade our interior lives before He can be truthfully present in our exterior actions. For that to happen, we must make the effort to care for our inward lives in solitude. If His love does not take root, Paul reminds us that we have gained nothing: "If I give away all I have, and if I deliver up my body to be burned, but have not love, I gain nothing" (1 Corinthians 13:3). Self-denial, then, must not exist separate from our inward reality, and that reality is nurtured in solitude. If we aren't careful, all of us can quickly slip into falseness and the temptation of wanting to be known. Solitude, then, is the fruitful place where that true growth can occur. We seek God patiently, and then our values and priorities begin to inwardly reflect His.

Certainly solitude isn't the only place such growth happens; we experience God in many contexts, including relationship and communities. But solitude is something we're especially likely to miss in our hurried lives. And like self-denial, it is a particularly consistent thread in our spiritual tradition, going all the way back to Jesus's retreat into the wilderness (see Matthew 4:1) and His solitary prayer in the Garden of Gethsemane (see Matthew 26:36–44). Even with the best of intentions, we can lose solitude in our busy, modern schedules. Likewise, in our pursuit of marriage, we can forget the spiritual usefulness of solitude. For many of us, it is the strength and power of our relational hopes that drown out our desire to be still and know that God is God. To say this is not to disparage marriage, but only to keep it in the tension we find between Ephesians 5 and 1 Corinthians 7.

In my experience, solitude helps me seek God first, in the quiet truth when I am alone before Him. Is He enough to hold my attention? If I'm not actively attentive to Him, I find that I miss His presence in the details of my activities, even if they are good activities. It sounds like a contradiction, but I can easily become too busy serving God in ministry to actually spend time with Him. I can get so busy with noble temporal tasks that I fail to be still before the eternal.

And perhaps we could say something similar about marriage. Maybe it's the very magnetism of romantic love that makes it all the more difficult for us to pay the needed attention to our souls, to our inward lives. As a married friend confided to me, it's much more difficult for him to find time alone with God now because it comes at the cost of time with his wife. This would be true of any commitment of ours, of course, but the challenge can be greater when it comes to a loved one.

Marital status alone will hardly predict whether a person knows something about solitude, and often it may be a loved one who inspires us toward quiet with God. To be sure, singles may in fact be guiltier of brushing aside the value of being alone with God. One can have unlimited hours available for God and yet still fail to direct those hours toward Him. Whereas the married person might be split between spouse and family, many single adults are often distracted by relatively trivial things—ambition, casual dating, time-wasters—and look far more self-indulgent by comparison. And this, in my opinion, is probably another reason why so many Christian singles get nudged down the aisle.

At any rate, regardless of marital status, solitude takes both effort and patience. I think if we are patient with solitude, and if we persevere through the initial struggle to remain still, we will gradually begin to want it more. As Merton described it, "Once God has called you to solitude, everything you touch leads you further into solitude."[7] Our growth may not always develop perfectly in one direction, but patience toward Him will increasingly cast our lives into new and different light.

Slowly, solitude starts to become a desire rather than a duty. It may feel like inner chaos at first, but soon it will start to feel like a gift.

As I thought about my own busyness in the months after Claire and I broke up, I couldn't help but wonder what I had missed in my reluctance to be still. What might God have revealed to me had I stopped moving?

I'm not sure I have the answer now, but I would have been wiser to remain in place. Rather than patching up loneliness with busyness, I could have sat still and listened.

And he said, "Go out and stand on the mount before the LORD." And behold, the LORD passed by, and a great and strong wind tore the mountains and broke in pieces the rocks before the LORD, but the LORD was not in the wind. And after the wind an earthquake, but the LORD was not in the earthquake. And after the earthquake a fire, but the LORD was not in the fire. And after the fire the sound of a low whisper.

—1 Kings 19:11–12

Blessed are the ears that gladly receive the pulses of the divine whisper, and give no heed to the many whisperings of this world.

Blessed indeed are those ears which hearken not to the voice which is sounding without, but unto the truth teaching inwardly.

—Thomas à Kempis

In the few days after our empanada picnic in Central Park, Eli and I found ourselves spending a lot of time together. We had dinner with my friends in the East Village. We hit up my favorite bar in Greenwich and waited in line for burgers at Shake Shack. We drank PBRs and played Scrabble. I was seeing far more of Eli than I had expected.

But just as quickly as we were hurled back into each other's company, Eli had to rush off to become a rock star. Literally. For part of his post-law-school year, he was going on tour with his friends' band as their guitar player. (The tour was perhaps one you've heard of—headlined by a group of brothers called Hanson.) We said good-bye late at night before his morning departure, and once again I adjusted to life without him.

Over the ensuing months, I was plodding along at my nine-to-five life while Eli was playing shows to crowds of screaming girls. It seemed a little unfair. But even though he was on the road, traveling in a cramped, smelly bus, we kept in touch. Each phone call, e-mail, or text was a more solid step toward friendship. It was also a reminder of what I didn't have: Eli, all to myself.

During one of our conversations, I asked one of my customary questions: "Any chance you'll be visiting any time soon?"

"Actually, yeah," he replied. I wasn't expecting that answer.

Before I knew it, Eli was in New York yet again. This time, however, it was more complicated because I had another friend in town—a boy in fact, but that is another story—and so it was a little while before Eli and I finally met up for dinner on one of his last nights in town.

Okay, so maybe I should talk about this other boy, though I'd sorta rather not. The short of it is we met in Chicago when I was out there visiting friends. We hit it off—I thought he was ridiculously cute—and kept in touch afterward. Then suddenly, this tall, handsome boy made plans to come out to New York to visit me. (Sounds familiar, no?) This guy was a catch: attractive, a Christian, an amazing cook. We had a fabulous week together, hanging out and getting to know each other. But I wasn't being fair to him because always in the back of my mind was Eli.

At the end of this gentleman's time in Brooklyn, I froze. He sweetly expressed his interest in carrying on what we had started. But I was not interested. I knew I had led him on, having been swept away by the week. But when faced with the reality of things, I had to own up to my mistake.

I was at a crisis. I was confused, sad, and guilty. My unluckiness in love continued. I slunk into self-pity and self-reproach. The conclusion of that week shouldn't have been so distressing, but it had exposed the blisters in my heart and then dabbed a little salt in them. Suddenly I missed Eli more than I had allowed myself to admit. But things hadn't worked out with Eli, and now they hadn't worked out with this other fine man, so what was wrong with me? I began once again to reconcile myself to a life alone. At the same time, I felt the smallest speck of hope that maybe I was meant to be with Eli after all. Singleness and marriage were on my mind with fresh urgency.

The day after this handsome suitor left, I walked to meet Eli for dinner. I dragged the baggage of not only that week, but also the residue that had built up around my affections for him. I arrived with all my defenses down and my heart rubbed raw. We sat at our table, ordered our *arepas,* and in typical fashion picked things up wherever they had left off.

It was a relief to be with Eli. With him, things were so natural and easy. We talked of this and that. I didn't have to pretend to be someone. I didn't have to work at conversation.

After the waitress refilled our water glasses, Eli's expression suddenly looked serious. And a little sheepish.

"So I had something I wanted to float by you," he said.

"Okay…"

"And it might be a little weird to bring up, given our history."

I tried to not jump to any conclusions.

"I've been thinking a lot about marriage lately."

"Uh-huh…"

"And I got this crazy idea."

My head started to spin.

"I want to write a book about it. More a book about why people might not get married."

Um, what? "A book about why people might not get married?" I asked, recovering my senses.

"Yeah, it would be sort of a biblical question mark for marriage. I mean, think about it: Why are we all so marriage-centric? Why aren't we better at loving our neighbors?"

I paused to process what he had just said, taking a big bite of food and chewing it slowly. After I overcame my initial surprise, I began to consider the idea seriously. Then it clicked. Not just the idea of the book itself, but everything: The past week, the way I had approached past relationships, the way I thought about singleness, the uneasiness I had felt about what I had been taught and its applications for my life as a single woman.

During the rest of dinner, we explored the topic. The more we talked about it, the more excited we became. I was surprised to discover how much interest I had for the idea. Then, as cautiously and unpresumptively as I could, I offered my services should he need any assistance with the project.

He promptly accepted.

So there we were, ex-boyfriend and ex-girlfriend writing a book about singleness, marriage, and love…together.

I know, I know. What were we thinking?

I had barely a moment to breathe before I fell headlong into writing a book, about love, with my ex-girlfriend. Not the smoothest move, reader.

In my defense, however, what else could I have done but fall prey to this timeless tale: Girl writes theological article; boy forms theo-crush; boy starts website, hassles girl for publicity; boy travels eight hundred miles for blind date with girl. Boy likes girl; girl (slowly!) warms up to boy; boy and girl date across cyberspace and telephone wires; boy and girl break up; and then—narrative triumph!—ex-boyfriend and ex-girlfriend write a book about marriage together!

A story for the ages! Right?

What was I thinking?

Allow me to explain.

The dinner in New York hadn't sprung up out of the blue; it was more like another step in a series of unlikely steps. The questions of the book had loomed in my mind for some time, and I had been in lengthy discussions on the topic of marriage with a variety of people I knew and respected: my parents, married friends, single friends, and others across the relational and theological spectrum. And yet the frayed strands never felt quite unified enough to put into words. They felt like a hunch, vague and ethereal. But then one day, several things coalesced and drew the questions to a point for me. For the first time, I felt that writing down my thoughts might be useful.

I was no author, nor did I have aspirations to be. I was a lawyer. But Claire worked for a publishing house, so it seemed natural to ask for her opinion. As part of her job, she reviewed manuscripts and book proposals, so I thought she could at least help me tease out the good ideas from the bad.

Given our history, I was reluctant to bring up the idea. We had broken up less than a year before, and we were only now finding our bearings as friends. Like most relationships, it had taken time for us to shift into a new gear, and I wasn't sure enough time had passed to even approach a conversation like this. I didn't want to ruin the new closeness between us.

And yet I knew she and I had tread much of this ground together, so it wasn't only her professional judgment I sought; I wanted to know what she thought of all this as my friend. Was I crazy to ask questions like these?

And so, cautiously and with much trepidation, I floated the concept of the book.

I am still amazed by how that evening went. As regretful as I had felt about what love meant between Claire and me while dating—a love that often meant calculated giving and taking—this was a bright exception. Whereas many relationships I had seen ended in antagonism and distrust, things between Claire and me had taken a better turn. We hadn't treated each other perfectly by any means, and yet the care we felt for each other extended beyond the outcome at hand. Kindness hadn't been limited to our status as a couple; kindness persisted. And that resembled something a bit closer to love.

In a way, our discussion that night felt like a form of forgiveness in motion, even if it wasn't complete. Claire and I hadn't done each other any grievous harm during our time together—at least not in the typical ways—and yet in a thousand moments between breakup and book, anger and distrust could have crept in and ruined the openness between us.

As far as I could tell, this kind of anger and distrust was extremely common in the relationships around me, for both non-Christians and Christians alike. Post-breakup forgiveness was thought of as either naïve or unrealistic, and so many of us chose not to step into its pain and loss of control. The Christian vision and power of forgiveness was submerged beneath "the way things go."

And indeed, anger and distrust were all-too-common features of the way things had gone in my own relationships. I had generally done little to prevent anger from sinking into my heart, and each time it did, it grew quickly into a sickness that ate away at my insides, making wreckage of relationships where there had once been beauty.

With Claire, though, it had been different. Both of us had taken an early step toward forgiveness, and I think we had done a pretty strong job of staying committed to it, even when it was rough. Neither of us forgave perfectly, but forgiveness was unquestionably our aim.

The relationship that lasted between Claire and me was perhaps a small picture of forgiveness overall. But as I think about it now, the principle at work beneath it was larger and more meaningful than I realized at the time. In the aftermath of our breakup, we had begun to step toward a love that was larger than ourselves.

LOVE AND FORGIVENESS

Love necessitates forgiveness. Forgiveness is a necessary movement of love. We cannot love our neighbor without forgiveness, and we cannot love truthfully without letting go. Were it not for our little gesture of forgiveness, a small fragment of love, Claire and I would never have had that conversation that night. We would have parted ways for good—and probably with more than a few lingering grudges.

The more I've thought about forgiveness, the more one thing has become clear to me: forgiveness requires work, and I always underestimate how much. I cannot know love when my heart remains an archive of wrongs. To remain at peace with others, to remain capable of active love, I have to actually change my inward posture in relation to others. I cannot commit to a vague forgiveness. I must actually forgive, and forgive as I have been forgiven. And this is all easier to *say* than to *do*.

Forgiveness had been abstract in many of my past relationships, and that was unfortunate, because what I often needed most was forgiveness, vibrant and alive. Forgiveness was not meant to be only gazed at from a distance; it was to be embodied. And Jesus couldn't have been clearer on this point: "So if you are offering your gift at the altar and there remember that your brother has something against you, leave your gift there before the altar and go. First be reconciled to your brother, and then come and offer your gift" (Matthew 5:23–24). And then even on the cross, hanging in the suffering of his own forgiveness, he cried out: "Father, forgive them, for they know not what they do" (Luke 23:34). Forgiveness is concrete.

I was only beginning to know a shadow of forgiveness, and yet I knew that if I was to live in His love, I had little choice but to forgive in view of my own need to be forgiven, and in view of my own dark capacity to wrong those around me. And so while Claire and I were a mere speck of what forgiveness could be in a relationship, it was something we got more right than we probably knew at the time. We chose forgiveness over self-preservation, and we stuck with it. And that was a form of love.

And the beautiful thing is this: forgiveness flowered into something unexpected.

After Claire listened to me explain the idea, I was amazed by her response: she wanted to explore the idea together. My hope had been that she wouldn't think the idea absurd, and now we were talking about writing a book. I could barely believe my ears.

And so we set to work, reading deeper on the topic and starting to put our pens to paper. As I left New York, e-mails once again sped through cyberspace. We talked about what direction we wanted the book to go and how we would get it done. We asked each other difficult questions about obedience and discipleship. We talked openly about our relationship, what we had done right and what we had missed. And we talked an awful lot about love.

Forgiveness breaks the chain of causality because he who "forgives" you—out of love—takes upon himself the consequences of what *you* have done. Forgiveness, therefore, always entails a sacrifice.

The price you must pay for your own liberation through another's sacrifice is that you in turn must be willing to liberate in the same way, irrespective of the consequences to yourself.

—Dag Hammarskjöld

For if you forgive others their trespasses, your heavenly Father will also forgive you, but if you do not forgive others their trespasses, neither will your Father forgive your trespasses.

—Matthew 6:14–15

As I meandered through the chapels, halls, and fortress walls, a singular beauty surrounded me: the gardens, the encased rosary bead, the unicorn tapestries, the landscape, the glorious weather. I was in the folds of majesty.

That afternoon I had retreated to the top of Manhattan for a day of rummaging through the Cloisters, a reconstructed monastery perched on a stunning precipice overlooking the Hudson River. I came there to gather myself. I hoped the A train would bring me to a moment of peace, revelation, and restoration.

Strolling through the Cloisters, however, I found it difficult to enter the space the structures were meant to create and which I was so desperate for. Its artifice kept nagging me. The tourists, the signs asking me not to touch, the guards: they all reminded me that I was not a pilgrim but a day-tripper. Unlike the monks and artists who had constructed its walls, I had hardly lived a life oriented toward prayer and solitude. Heck, I was patting myself on the back for a fifty-minute commute toward one day of sustained quiet.

But I knew that even a day would do me good. I needed to get away from the book. Everything had thickened. For months, Eli and I had been digging into the subject, and I was getting buried under the debris. I was losing myself. During that week, it had been particularly heavy.

I went into the project excited and confident. I had a lot I wanted to say and a lot I wanted to learn. But soon a simple idea over dinner became a cataclysmic shift that started to fracture my complacency. It was unsettling. How could my love have been so askew for so long? How was I going to start living differently in light of what I was learning? How could I untangle my heart? I wasn't up for the challenge that was now before me.

When I walked into the Cloisters, feeling like a flat stick figure amid the centuries of spirituality that had come before me, I was more agitated than soothed. I was encouraged but also discouraged by the examples of lives lived for God. At every turn, the phony marks of tourism reminded me that I had lived my life with as much commitment to love as a mere visitor. For so long I had cheapened the extravagant vision of God's love with labels, tied it off with ropes, and studied it as an artifact rather than as a living emblem of truth.

Writing this book has been a long, hard process, personally, spiritually, relationally, artistically. I think Eli would agree. But the very challenge of it has been one of the greatest blessings. It has forced me to dig down and burrow in for the long haul, to realize Christ not only called us to salvation but also to our cross. It has pushed me beyond the Please Do Not Touch signs. It has brought Eli and me closer through many hard and sometimes unpleasant conversations. It has taken away from me every idea and identity I thought I owned and has reminded me of this rough paraphrase of something A. W. Tozer wrote: As long as we imagine we own anything, that thing owns us. As soon as we know that we own nothing, then God owns us.

Nothing has unsettled me more, and thus nothing has made more room in my heart for Christ to usher in His love.

The wind combed the long weeds and golden wildflowers over the rocky coastline of Morro Bay, California. On our way back from dinner, we parked the car on the side of the road and stepped down into the unruly field that led to the sea. As Eli walked ahead on a narrow path through the brush, I hung back and pulled out my camera. The yellow foreground was just a preamble to the rugged, beryl coast. Eli entered the landscape like a brush stroke. I snapped a picture.

This was my second trip out to California in a month's time. Since our dinner in Brooklyn when the book idea first materialized, Eli and I had been writing ceaselessly, discussing and researching. But we were most productive when we were together, and so I left noisy New York to join him in California for a week of solid work, and then for another.

On this particular evening, after a satisfying day of writing, Eli drove me to a small town just north of where we were working and took me out to dinner. Over our messy burgers, we talked more about the project and our friendship. It was amazing to see how far I had come since I saw my first shooting star. Not only did I know Eli on a much deeper level, and not only had he become so much more to me than a potential mate, but our understanding of discipleship had been enlarged.

Together, as we studied the Gospels and sat at the feet of some of the greatest Christian minds, as we wrangled our relational habits and challenged our previously unchallenged assumptions, what materialized wasn't a formula for dating or marriage but Christ's rich vision of love.

As I stood with my camera around my neck and watched Eli walking toward the waves, I realized how curious it was that such a dramatic landscape—waves crashing against cliffs and wind tangling overgrown grass—could create an effect of serenity. It was so much more than a matter of perspective; it was a case of wholeness. Because the scene was complete—including the gamut of natural elements from sky to sea to grass, green to blue to white—it was harmonious despite its individual details of chaos.

Throughout my evangelical upbringing, I had trained myself to look ahead but focus only on a few elements. For example, I homed in on the uncertainties of marriage or the topsy-turviness of navigating the single life. With each guy I dated, I ran straight for the cliff, neglecting the wider panorama. Or I tripped in the weeds, failing to look up at the beautiful coast ahead. Intellectually, I knew the essence of the Christian life, but I was a clumsy fool when it came to embodying it. I had anatomized Christian love and sorted out its parts like a butcher. In doing so, I had killed it.

In particular, my pursuit of marriage had caused me to lose sight of my neighbor. And inevitably, I was not content or composed. I was not pursuing the gospel, but a Christianized version of the American dream. It was another form of worked-up selfishness.

But as I stood in the coastal grasses of Morro Bay, I was content. Working side-by-side with Eli to pursue a more complete vision of discipleship, I was beginning to realize the simple, transformative love that Christ modeled in my own life. I was learning to look around me without stressing over whether the rough rocks or the disheveled ground was the path before me. I simply saw the expanse of God's goodness in both, and in everything beyond them.

I smiled to myself and ran to catch up with Eli.

A CONCLUSION

And that's our story.

We met, we dated, we broke up, and then we wrote a book that questioned our own focus on marriage, together. If that sounds a bit confusing to you, trust us, it is. We're not sure we'd recommend it.

Our story was, in a way, the first domino in the cascade that brought us here to you, reader, to the thesis, and to the possibility that marriage was less of a linchpin to Christianity than we initially thought. Our story was an example of how things go in the average relationship, and also a reason why we don't think that's necessarily all that much to admire. We did most of what we had been told, and yet we knew little of the life and vitality of Christ's transformative love.

We know we've jumped around and covered a lot of ground, so here is a quick restatement of what we saw in our churches and communities:

1. Christians grow up in the midst of two powerful pressure points: (a) widespread marriage-happiness inside the church, and (b) an exaltation of individualism and romance outside the church. Not surprisingly, many of us have a difficult time untangling the two.

2. We spend major amounts of our formative years looking for a spouse. Far from the example of Christ's love, we seek one

person who will meet our hopes and expectations. Before we consider what it might mean to love our neighbor, we have thought extensively about what will qualify another person for our love.

3. If we find a potential spouse, then our relationship all too often operates on roughly the same terms as those practiced in society, with a few extra purity requirements tacked on (which, if the studies are to be trusted, are poorly observed).

4. If we get married, we proceed on to seminars. If we don't, we break up and return to the search. All the while, singleness lingers in the background as an object of acute anxiety, in contrast to significant biblical witness to the contrary.

And those were roughly the habits of our communities, and of our relationship as well.

We both were quick to seek what we wanted, but slow to remember love. We did things right but got it wrong. We were intentional with each other. We rarely fought. In at least one sense, our relationship was a picture of the best practices we had known from our teen and college years. Yet even though we navigated that fairly well, we still missed love. Our love was largely indistinguishable from that of the world.

And love's absence could be seen in many details throughout our story. If we had known love, we would have treated each other as more than just marital candidates. If we had known love, we would have been less trapped in the relentless accounting between expectation and reality, and less quick to keep tally of what qualities the other person was missing. If we had known love, we would have been mindful of the dissonance between the needs of our neighbors and the complete spousal myopia that dominated our vision.

How love might have changed the story of Claire and Eli is a mystery to us, and yet love certainly would have meant something beyond what we knew, something more firm and rooted than the wandering of our conditional love.

But the irony of our story is this, and we would be unwise to ignore it: without Claire or Eli, there probably would have been no book. We have each other to thank, albeit indirectly, for love's vitality in our lives, and it is a gift we wouldn't trade for anything. God was the final Author and Origin of love in our lives, and yet it was a piece of romantic fan mail He used to bring us to it.

Who knows where things will go from here.

And truly, if you're like us, you probably prefer a tidy, clean ending to the story. As do we. We like to hear how Jesus healed the bleeding woman but not how the "rich young man" was told to sell all he owned. We like to hear about the Christian football star, but not about the pastor in the small town who gave up a promising career. We like to hear how Jesus brought a couple together, but not how He kept them apart.

Here's the thing, though: Christ promises no such tidy ending. Following Jesus will bring us into a life that is newly abundant, yes, but He will also bring great uncertainty to our plans. We can hardly say we've followed Him with everything if we rule out the possibility He would ask us to do anything contrary to The Plan.

Though we often view Christ as an accessory to our lives, He should in fact be much, *much* more. Christ ought to be the central and orienting fact of our being. We must place every detail of our lives into His capable hands, and we must not turn back. Our surrender must include everything, and exempt nothing.

Indeed, we regularly remind ourselves that His yoke is easy and His burden is light. But we are less likely to recall that Jesus also said, "Enter by the narrow gate" (Matthew 7:13) and "If anyone would come after me, let him deny himself and take up his cross daily and follow me" (Luke 9:23). It is one thing to hear these words, and another to humble

ourselves beneath them and allow them to reorient our self-guided existence. Jesus was clear on this point: we must listen to His words and then
hear, obey, and follow. As Bonhoeffer declared, nothing short of simple
obedience will do.[1]

Now don't misread this, because we aren't saying that following
Christ will mean any one outcome for your particular marriage prospects.
We cannot suggest where God will lead *you,* and to paraphrase something
Augustine said, God will always prefer obedience over any specific status,
whether married or single. Obedience is more important. Grace, and obedience (in response to grace), is our position before God, not marriage or
singleness.

And truly, if status even sounds like the point, we have failed to persuade you of anything worthwhile in the end. A focus on status apart
from obedience inevitably leads us to pride and legalism, and we are not
to boast in anything but Christ (see Galatians 6:14). When we behave to
be seen, acting out of pride, we are opposed by God (see Luke 18:13–14;
James 4:6; 1 Peter 5:5). How *your* life will look as a follower of Christ is
not for us to prescribe, of course, but rather for the Lord. It is to be worked
out with great diligence.

In short, if we leave you with two thoughts, let them be these.

First, if we continue to try to fit love into our own, often cultural,
understanding of marriage, we have almost certainly missed the fullness
of Christ's teachings on love.

And second, we must not underestimate the task at hand. To follow
Christ, we must lose our lives to gain them. To love God with all our
heart, soul, mind, and strength, and to love our neighbor as ourselves, we
must deny ourselves and take up our crosses daily.

That is how we love.

So if there is any encouragement in Christ, any comfort from love, any participation in the Spirit, any affection and sympathy, complete my joy by being of the same mind, having the same love, being in full accord and of one mind. Do nothing from selfish ambition or conceit, but in humility count others more significant than yourselves. Let each of you look not only to his own interests, but also to the interests of others. Have this mind among yourselves, which is yours in Christ Jesus, who, though he was in the form of God, did not count equality with God a thing to be grasped, but emptied himself, by taking the form of a servant, being born in the likeness of men. And being found in human form, he humbled himself by becoming obedient to the point of death, even death on a cross.

—Philippians 2:1–8

QUESTIONS AND ANSWERS

Q: **Why don't you give more practical advice in the book?**

Eli: The short answer is that we're hardly the best people to give dating or marriage advice. We are not marriage or family experts, nor are we pastors, and those folks have a lot more practical wisdom to offer. Because we can't say how a person should navigate marriage or how someone should lead a local church, we've made great effort to not speak loosely on those topics. As congregants and readers, we tried to highlight issues where we thought we could add a helpful word. But if someone has questions about the applications of this, we'd much rather tell that person to be prayerful and seek the Lord in solitude, as well as the counsel of pastors and leaders in his or her own community. We wouldn't have written this book if we didn't have something to say, but we know that experience and sensitivity to one's particular context—which we of course cannot speak to—is super important.

Instead, what we tried to do here is to wrestle with what it means to "lose our life to gain it" and "take up our cross daily," both in general and in the context of relationships. While that might not seem immediately practical—in the way we sometimes say "practical"—we hope that with prayer and thoughtfulness, it will change all sorts of practical things in the lives of those who seek it.

Q: **Why the pseudonyms?**

Claire: Google.

Eli: What she means is that we wanted to preserve the mystery of our own story because our story isn't about the ending, happy or sad. Unfortunately, Google doesn't leave room for much mystery these days.

Claire: Plus, the story, though ours, isn't only about us. It could be anybody's story. Many Christians meet, start dating, and then grapple with the same questions that Eli and I had. The point here isn't so much our particular story as it is about the general landscape of these issues and, more importantly, the God that extends beyond them to a kingdom that is not our own.

Q: **What would you say about the Genesis account? What about the fact that there are two genders? Isn't gender (and therefore marriage) a fundamental part of who we are?**

Eli: Yes, definitely. Clearly gender is an incredibly important part of our identity as created beings. If the sexes weren't of such consequence, then the debate over sexuality and family wouldn't have raged in Christianity for two thousand years. We don't deny that there is something deeply meaningful about the way the genders relate, and in the mystery and beauty of family.

But it's important to remember that the greatest commandment nevertheless orients our lives primarily around a love for God and for our *neighbor,* not only family.

Of course, we wouldn't want to say anything that diminishes the importance of the Genesis account. We just think some of the marriage sermons should not *exclusively* focus on Genesis 1 and 2 and Ephesians 5, but rather dive into some of the other passages as well.

Q: What about procreation? Doesn't the fact that God commands us to procreate support marriage?

Eli: Yes, it does. But Paul and Jesus were aware of that too, and they still said the things they said. And both remained single.

Claire: Also, here is some extra food for thought. This is a quote from Rodney Clapp, author of *Families at the Crossroads,* on the unique symbol presented by the life of a single—and childless—Christian: "The single Christian ultimately *must* trust in the resurrection. The married, after all, can fall back on the passage of the family name to children, and on being remembered by children. But singles mount the high wire of faith without the net of children and their memory. If singles live on, it will be because there is resurrection. And if they are remembered, they will be remembered by the family called church."[1] Barry Danylak also makes the same point in a longer study in *Redeeming Singleness,* another great book, as does Albert Hsu in his excellent *Singles at the Crossroads.*

Q: What about studies that say Christian kids are sleeping around more than ever now?

Eli: Without a doubt, we need to take Paul seriously in 1 Corinthians 7:9. It *is* better to marry than to burn with passion, and that will mean marriage in many cases. Nothing said here should discount that.

Yet at the same time, in our view, some of the sex studies miss the point. Yes, Christians are sleeping around and that's not all right. Not only is it not okay but it also reveals a gap between who we are and who we say we are. But simply not having sex won't fix the deeper issue. It is one thing to be hypocritical—saying you're devoted to Christ while doing what you want—but it is far more grave to miss love, *to miss the feature Christ said would characterize our lives in Him.* That doesn't mean Christ isn't interested in both issues—it's not one or the other—but it does mean that love is very, very important and that sometimes we fret more about sexuality than about Christlikeness in a broader sense (which includes sexuality).

To take it even a step further, what if for each study released on how many kids are sleeping around, there was a parallel study on how many of us don't really know love, that is, how many of us had been unfaithful to Christian love in its basic implications? Such a study would be impossible to pull off, but it would be pretty interesting to see the results side by side.

Q: **What about the "Don't commit adultery" command in the Ten Commandments? Doesn't that lend some importance and sanctity to marriage?**

Eli: It does, but a command from God that says not to break the rules of marriage is different from God telling you to get married. If someone tells you not to steal, you don't think that person told you to go out and shop.

Q: **Okay, so if it were up to you, which other verses in the Bible should we also be discussing in our marriage and family seminars?**

Eli and Claire: Well, it's not a perfect list, but we did think of at least seven sermons that we'd be curious to hear from the pulpit. Any pulpit.

- "Heaven on Earth: The Absence of Marriage in Heaven" (Matthew 22)
- "Single Christian Leaders in the New Testament: Christ, Paul, and John the Baptist"
- "I have married a wife, and therefore I cannot come," aka "Missing the Banquet for Marriage" (Luke 14:15–24)
- "Paul's Marriage Counsel: Avoid It If You Can" (1 Corinthians 7)
- "144,000...Virgins?" (Revelation 14)
- "Not Only for Weddings" (1 Corinthians 13)
- "The Good Ol' Days? Patriarchs and Polygamy"

Q: But still, doesn't the Bible say an awful lot about marriage and family? Doesn't that say something?

Eli and Claire: In the Old Testament, yes, it does say quite a bit. But have you ever considered how many dysfunctional marriages there were? Try to think of one healthy marriage in the OT. Even if family played a major role in the OT, that doesn't necessarily mean it supports today's particular (perhaps cultural) emphasis on "healthy" families, which may be a distinct concern in certain regards. (This is not to say "healthy" families are a problem, which would be silly, but only that a cultural vision of healthiness isn't as primary as a biblical vision of love or obedience.)

In short, we're of the opinion that the New Testament treatment of marriage is fairly minimal, at least in relation to how we often think about it. And truly, if you reread the NT now with this lens applied— that maybe Jesus was less worked up about marriage than we are—we think you might see the same thing.

The point of course isn't to say that we shouldn't apply Christ's teachings to our marriages—because we should—but rather that we should listen to the fullness of what He said, not filter it through our modern understanding of marriage.

Q: What about attraction and desire? Doesn't the fact that we're attracted to other people mean something?

Eli and Claire: Certainly it does. And we should acknowledge fully the God-given beauty and incomprehensibility of attraction—the thrill of a face, the beauty of an attitude, the *something* that evades language. Nothing about love requires us to ignore the truth of how things are, and how mysterious it is that we are drawn to others so deeply. Contrary to the Gnostics or the extreme ascetics, nothing about love prevents us from finding wonder in the good and beautiful gift God created in relationship.

And yet at the same time, love reminds us that our commitment to others must go beyond the pleasure and beauty they offer us—to encompass the ungrateful spouse, the difficult coworker, the friend who betrays us. In all these, love allows us to see and appreciate the beauty in how we relate, then beckons us to stick around once the beauty (inevitably) fades.

As our shared-literary-crush Marilynne Robinson put it: "The antidote to fear, distrust, self-interest is always loyalty.... This is utopian. And yet. Certainly it describes something of which many of us feel deprived. We have reasoned our way to uniformly conditional relationships.... We have instead decided to respect our parents, maybe, if they meet our stringent standards of deserving. Just so do our children respect us, maybe."[2] And the result? "I think this may contribute enormously to the sadness so many of us feel at the heart of contemporary society."

Q: **What about the fact that parenthood teaches you how to love?**

Claire: It does, and nothing we say here should diminish that. Parenthood certainly expands one's ability to love selflessly, and it can be an amazing metaphor to help us understand how God, our heavenly Father, relates to us.

Q: **What about the fact that lots of single people are selfish?**

Eli: It's true. Single people are often very selfish. And yet our suggestion is that sometimes the fear of single selfishness has become so large in the evangelical mind that we talk as if marriage provided a categorical elimination of selfishness. It doesn't (and fairly strong evidence of this can be seen in the not terribly great evangelical divorce rate).

Reality is more complicated. Single and married persons alike must learn to love, and we all must grow up and out of cramped self-rule. This is the way of the Cross, and the Cross is available to anyone who follows Christ and is ready to deny themselves, whatever their status. Marriage will provide reinforcement for growth in this area, to be sure, but neither the status of marriage nor singleness is a guarantee of growth in love. And some of the marriage buzz misses this, I think.

It is also worth noting here that we never said people should stay single because singleness allows them to do what they want. In our view, the idea that life is about self is exactly the kind of vision that undermines both marriage (i.e., a spouse becomes a means to achieve happiness) *and* singleness (i.e., people stay single for the sake of self-indulgence). Neither is consistent with the idea of losing one's life to gain it, nor with the requirements of love overall.

Q: The Hanson brothers. Really?

Eli: It was a curious time in my life.

Q: And do they...?

Eli: Yes, they still play "MmmBop."

Q: Okay, but seriously now, what's your deal? You guys wrote a book that questions marriage, *together.* How does that work?

Claire: With lots of bicker-editing. In fact, cowriting is kinda like being in a marriage.

Eli: Delicately.

Q: And where exactly are you two relationally?

Claire: Oh, look at the time!

Eli: Thanks for reading, guys!

APPENDIX

LOVE

Put on then, as God's chosen ones, holy and beloved, compassionate hearts, kindness, humility, meekness, and patience, bearing with one another and, if one has a complaint against another, forgiving each other; as the Lord has forgiven you, so you also must forgive. And above all these put on love, which binds everything together in perfect harmony. (Colossians 3:12–14)

———

Therefore be imitators of God, as beloved children. And walk in love, as Christ loved us and gave himself up for us, a fragrant offering and sacrifice to God. (Ephesians 5:1–2)

———

Now may our God and Father himself, and our Lord Jesus, direct our way to you, and may the Lord make you increase and abound in love for one another and for all, as we do for you, so that he may establish your hearts blameless in holiness before our God and Father, at the coming of our Lord Jesus with all his saints. (1 Thessalonians 3:11–13)

———

For this reason I remind you to fan into flame the gift of God, which is in you through the laying on of my hands, for God gave us a spirit not of fear but of power and love and self-control. (2 Timothy 1:6–7)

———

His divine power has granted to us all things that pertain to life and godliness, through the knowledge of him who called us to his own glory and excellence, by which he has granted to us his precious and very great promises, so that through them you may become partakers of the divine nature, having escaped from the corruption that is in the world because of sinful desire. For this very reason, make every effort to supplement your faith with virtue, and virtue with knowledge, and knowledge with self-control, and self-control with steadfastness, and steadfastness with godliness, and godliness with brotherly affection, and brotherly affection with love. For if these qualities are yours and are increasing, they keep you from being ineffective or unfruitful in the knowledge of our Lord Jesus Christ. (2 Peter 1:3–8)

Everyone who believes that Jesus is the Christ has been born of God, and everyone who loves the Father loves whoever has been born of him. By this we know that we love the children of God, when we love God and obey his commandments. For this is the love of God, that we keep his commandments. And his commandments are not burdensome. For everyone who has been born of God overcomes the world. And this is the victory that has overcome the world—our faith. (1 John 5:1–4)

By this it is evident who are the children of God, and who are the children of the devil: whoever does not practice righteousness is not of God, nor is the one who does not love his brother. (1 John 3:10)

Whoever says he is in the light and hates his brother is still in darkness. Whoever loves his brother abides in the light, and in him there is no cause for stumbling. But whoever hates his brother is in the darkness and walks in the darkness, and does not know where he is going, because the darkness has blinded his eyes. (1 John 2:9–11)

Now the works of the flesh are evident: sexual immorality, impurity, sensuality, idolatry, sorcery, enmity, strife, jealousy, fits of anger, rivalries, dissensions, divisions, envy, drunkenness, orgies, and things like these. I warn you, as I warned you before, that those who do such things will not inherit the kingdom of God. But the fruit of the Spirit is love, joy, peace, patience, kindness, goodness, faithfulness, gentleness, self-control; against such things there is no law. And those who belong to Christ Jesus have crucified the flesh with its passions and desires. (Galatians 5:19–24)

So flee youthful passions and pursue righteousness, faith, love, and peace, along with those who call on the Lord from a pure heart. (2 Timothy 2:22)

For you were called to freedom, brothers. Only do not use your freedom as an opportunity for the flesh, but through love serve one another. For the whole law is fulfilled in one word: "You shall love your neighbor as yourself." But if you bite and devour one another, watch out that you are not consumed by one another. (Galatians 5:13–15)

Owe no one anything, except to love each other, for the one who loves another has fulfilled the law. For the commandments, "You shall not commit adultery, You shall not murder, You shall not steal, You shall not covet," and any other commandment, are summed up in this word: "You shall love your neighbor as yourself." Love does no wrong to a neighbor; therefore love is the fulfilling of the law. (Romans 13:8–10)

But you must remember, beloved, the predictions of the apostles of our Lord Jesus Christ. They said to you, "In the last time there will be scoffers, following their own ungodly passions." It is these who cause divisions, worldly people, devoid of the Spirit. But you, beloved, building yourselves up in your most holy faith and praying in the Holy Spirit, keep yourselves in the love of God, waiting for the mercy of our Lord Jesus Christ that leads to eternal life. (Jude 1:17–21)

As I urged you when I was going to Macedonia, remain at Ephesus so that you may charge certain persons not to teach any different doctrine, nor to devote themselves to myths and endless genealogies, which promote speculations rather than the stewardship from God that is by faith. The aim of our charge is love that issues from a pure heart and a good conscience and a sincere faith. Certain persons, by swerving from these, have wandered away into vain discussion, desiring to be teachers of the law, without understanding either what they are saying or the things about which they make confident assertions. (1 Timothy 1:3–7)

Now concerning food offered to idols: we know that "all of us possess knowledge." This "knowledge" puffs up, but love builds up. If anyone imagines that he knows something, he does not yet know as he ought to know. But if anyone loves God, he is known by God. (1 Corinthians 8:1–3)

Follow the pattern of the sound words that you have heard from me, in the faith and love that are in Christ Jesus. By the Holy Spirit who dwells within us, guard the good deposit entrusted to you. (2 Timothy 1:13–14)

Let us hold fast the confession of our hope without wavering, for he who promised is faithful. And let us consider how to stir up one another to love and good works, not neglecting to meet together, as is the habit of some, but encouraging one another, and all the more as you see the Day drawing near. (Hebrews 10:23–25)

Beloved, let us love one another, for love is from God, and whoever loves has been born of God and knows God. Anyone who does not love does not know God, because God is love. In this the love of God was made manifest among us, that God sent his only Son into the world, so that we might live through him. In this is love, not that we have loved God but that he loved us and sent his Son to be the propitiation for our sins. Beloved, if God so loved us, we also ought to love one another. No one has ever seen God; if we love one another, God abides in us and his love is perfected in us.

By this we know that we abide in him and he in us, because he has given us of his Spirit. And we have seen and testify that the Father has sent his Son to be the Savior of the world. Whoever confesses that Jesus is the Son of God, God abides in him, and he in God. So we have come to know and to believe the love that God has for us. God is love, and whoever abides in love abides in God, and God abides in him. By this is love perfected with us, so that we may have confidence for the day of judgment, because as he is so also are we in this world. There is no fear in love, but perfect love casts out fear. For fear has to do with punishment, and whoever fears has not been perfected in love. We love because he first loved us. If anyone says, "I love God," and hates his brother, he is a liar; for he who does not love his brother whom he has seen cannot love God whom he has not seen. And this commandment we have from him: whoever loves God must also love his brother. (1 John 4:7–21)

I made known to them your name, and I will continue to make it known, that the love with which you have loved me may be in them, and I in them. (John 17:26)

As the Father has loved me, so have I loved you. Abide in my love. (John 15:9)

Discussion Questions

1. Do you think we tend to overemphasize marriage in evangelical culture? Why or why not?
2. What does it mean to love God with all your heart, soul, mind, and strength?
3. What does it mean to love your neighbor?
4. Who is your neighbor? (And by that, we mean your actual neighbor). List five. What would it mean to love them as you love yourself?
5. Eli looked to Bruce and Julie (from chapter 3) as an example of what it means to love a neighbor. What examples have you witnessed?
6. Why does love require the death of self?
7. What does it mean to deny yourself, take up your cross daily, and follow Christ?
8. In the relationships you are in now (friendship, dating, marriage, etc.), what would it mean to step toward Christ's manner of love? How would those relationships look different?
9. What does loneliness mean to you now? What could it mean?
10. Why is solitude neglected? Do you think solitude is underemphasized? Why or why not?
11. In what ways can you make more space for solitude in your life?
12. How does forgiveness relate to love? How does forgiveness enable love?

Acknowledgments

Many thanks to the following for feedback on early drafts and general awesomeness: Jenni Burke, Alice Crider, Ken Petersen, Vito Aiuto, Justin Anderson, Madhu Balasubramanium, Will and Kristin Bankston, Beidemariam and Freya Bekele, Mark Beuving, Chris Broesamle, Ashley Bruns, Rachael Butler, Rachel Cambell, Jeff Carver, Jimmy Chalk, Andrea Cheuk, Lucy Collins, Christine Colón, Chris Comstock, Carol Cornish, Gabe Cortez, Emily Curran, Barry Danylak, Jeff Davids, Bethany Davis, Chris and Anslee de Lastic, Elizabeth Dettori, Elizabeth Dishman, Brandon Ebel, Ryan Ellis, Jason Ellis, Julie Evans, Brandon Fischer, Sharon Forbes, Bruce and Julie Freeby, Nathan Gammie, Kristen Gaylord, Joe and Beyth Greenetz, Jon and Valerie Guerra, Jenny Hall, Joseph Hellerman, Wesley Hill, Kevin and Elaine Hill, Barbara Hungerford, Elizabeth Hunnicutt, Allison Hunter, Alan Jacobs, Genevieve Jenkins, John and Judy Jeter, Jordan Jolliff, Dan King, Tim Kirchner, Dan Koch, Carrie Koch, Kristie Koll, Ann Ku, Jacob Lin, Amanda and Mitch McGuffey, Calleigh McRaith, Eric Metaxas, Matt Miller, Ryan Miller, Donald Moline, Lynne Moll, Ryan Moore, Jana Otte, Sarah Painter, Jamey and Gretchen Pappas, Karen Paul, Daniel Payne, Lauren Peffley, Deborah Press, Elissa Rhodea, John Rotman, Evan and Kimberly Roullard, Erica Sauder, Matt Seodore, Sarah Shotwell, Cole Slinker, Garett and Amy Stapp, John Starke, Rhett Stonelake, Laura Sullivan, Nathan Sunukjian, Magda Tewes, Jay Thomas, Ken Van Vliet, Zach Ward, Gary Weyel, Carolinne White, Peter and Tammy Williams, John Wilson, Ryan Wilson, Brett Wise, Aimee Wong, Kevin Woodward, Vance Yarborough, Allen Yeh.

NOTES

Chapter 1: Purple Days

1. Andrew J. Cherlin, *The Marriage-Go-Round: The State of Marriage and the Family in America Today* (New York: Alfred A. Knopf, 2009).
2. Al Mohler, quoted in Erik Eckholm, "Umarried Pastor, Seeking Job, Sees Bias," *The New York Times,* March 21, 2011, www.nytimes.com/2011/03/22/us/22pastor.html?pagewanted=all.
3. *The Boundless Line* (blog), "About Us," Focus on the Family, www.boundless.org/2005/aboutus.cfm.
4. *Boundless,* "Featured Resources," review of *Get Married,* www.boundless.org/resources/.
5. Candice Watters, "Defending 'The Cost of Delaying Marriage,'" *Boundless,* www.boundless.org/2005/articles/a0001145.cfm.
6. Andreas Köstenberger, *God, Marriage, and Family: Rebuilding the Biblical Foundation,* 2nd ed. (Wheaton, IL: Crossway, 2010), 167.
7. Köstenberger, *God, Marriage, and Family,* 167.
8. Redeemer Presbyterian Church, "Redeemer Sermon Store," http://sermons.redeemer.com/store/index.cfm?fuseaction=category.display&category_ID=12.
9. For a nonexhaustive list of verses on love, see Appendix B.
10. Lauren F. Winner, *Real Sex: The Naked Truth About Chastity* (Grand Rapids, MI: Brazos Press, 2005), 25.
11. Christine A. Colón and Bonnie E. Field, *Singled Out: Why Celibacy Must Be Reinvented in Today's Church* (Grand Rapids, MI: Brazos Press, 2009), 11–12.
12. Debra Farrington, quoted in "Solitary Refinement" by Lauren F. Winner, *Christianity Today,* June 11, 2001, vol. 45, no. 8, www.christianitytoday.com/ct/2001/june11/1.30.html.

13. Mary Jo Weaver, "Single Blessedness," *Commonweal*, vol. 106 (October 26, 1979), 588–91.

14. Debbie Maken, *Getting Serious About Getting Married: Rethinking the Gift of Singleness* (Wheaton, IL: Crossway, 2006), 80.

15. Barry Danylak, *Redeeming Singleness: How the Storyline of Scripture Affirms the Single Life* (Wheaton, IL: Crossway, 2010), 19.

Chapter 2: Love Thy Neighbor

1. Dallas Willard, *Knowing Christ Today: Why We Can Trust Spiritual Knowledge* (New York: HarperOne, 2009), 92, emphasis in original.

2. Oswald Chambers, *My Utmost for His Highest* (Uhrichsville, OH: Barbour, 1935), 191.

3. John of the Cross, *The Collected Works of St. John of the Cross* (Washington, D.C.: Institute of Carmelite Studies, 1991), 90.

Chapter 4: Tattered Ledgers

1. Thomas Merton, *The Secular Journal of Thomas Merton* (New York: Farrar, Straus & Cudahy, 1959), 190.

2. George Herbert, "Love III," The Poetry Foundation, "Poems and Poets," www.poetryfoundation.org/poem/173632.

Chapter 5: Self-Denial and the Tyranny of Mine

1. A.W. Tozer, *The Pursuit of God* (Camp Hill, PA: Christian Publications, 1982), 22.

2. Fyodor Dostoevsky, *The Brothers Karamazov* (New York: Farrar, Straus and Giroux, 1990), 236.

Chapter 6: Those Who Have Flung Themselves

1. William James, *The Varieties of Religious Experience* (New York: Longmans, Green and Co., 1911), 321.

2. James, *Varieties of Religious Experience*, 324.

3. James, *Varieties of Religious Experience*, 359–61.

4. Thomas Merton, *The Wisdom of the Desert: Sayings from the Desert Fathers of the Fourth Century* (New York: New Directions, 1960), 5.

5. Richard J. Foster, *Freedom of Simplicity: Finding Harmony in a Complex World* (New York: HarperCollins, 1981), 66.

6. Thomas Merton, *Wisdom of the Desert*, 18.

7. Foster, *Freedom of Simplicity*, 70–71.

8. Merton, *Wisdom of the Desert*.

9. Merton, *Wisdom of the Desert*, 60.

10. Merton, *Wisdom of the Desert*, 67.

11. Helen Waddell, *The Desert Fathers* (New York: Vintage Spiritual Classics, 1998), 57.

12. James, *Varieties of Religious Experience*, 286.

13. Thomas à Kempis, *The Imitation of Christ* (New York: Vintage Spiritual Classics, 1998), 125.

14. John Calvin, *Golden Booklet of the True Christian Life* (Grand Rapids, MI: Baker Book House, 1952), 23.

Chapter 7: Focus Off the Family?

1. Joseph Hellerman, *When the Church Was a Family: Recapturing Jesus' Vision for Authentic Christian Community* (Nashville, TN: B&H, 2009), 55.

2. Hellerman, *When the Church Was a Family*, 56.

3. Stanley Hauerwas, *A Community of Character: Toward a Constructive Christian Social Ethic* (Notre Dame, IN: University of Notre Dame Press, 1981), 189.

4. Dietrich Bonhoeffer, *A Testament to Freedom: The Essential Writings of Dietrich Bonhoeffer*, ed. Geffrey B. Kelly and F. Burton Nelson (New York: HarperOne, 1995), 308.

5. Dietrich Bonhoeffer, *The Cost of Discipleship* (New York: Macmillan, 1959; Touchstone, 1995), 51. Citations refer to the Touchstone edition.

6. Bonhoeffer, *Cost of Discipleship*, 196–97.

7. Karl Barth, *Church Dogmatics*, vol. 4, no. 2 (n.p.: Continuum International Publishing Group, 2004), 551.

8. Bonhoeffer, *Cost of Discipleship*, 180–81.

Chapter 8: The Lost Chapter

1. Matthew Henry, *An Exposition of the Old and New Testament*, vol. V (New York: Robert Carter and Brothers, 1856), 361. (Also found in *Matthew Henry's Commentary on the Whole Bible*, www.biblestudy tools.com/commentaries/matthew-henry-complete/1-corinthians/7 .html?p=5).

2. Augustine, *Treatises on Marriage and Other Subjects* (New York: Fathers of the Church, Inc., 1955), 153.

3. Barry Danylak, *Redeeming Singleness: How the Storyline of Scripture Affirms the Single Life* (Wheaton, IL: Crossway, 2010), 211.

4. Stanley Hauerwas, *The Hauerwas Reader*, ed. John Berkman and Michael G. Cartwright, (Duke University Press, 2001), 497.

5. John Calvin, *Epistles of Paul the Apostle to the Corinthians*, vol. 1 (Edinburgh: The Calvin Translation Society, 1848), 253.

6. Craig Blomberg, *The NIV Application Commentary: 1 Corinthians* (Grand Rapids, MI: Zondervan, 1994), 122.

7. Matthew Henry, *An Exposition of the Old and New Testament*, 360.

8. John Wesley, *Explanatory Notes upon the New Testament* (London: Conference-Office, 14, City-Road, 1813), 80.

Chapter 9: Tips from Tolstoy

1. Ilya Tolstoy, *Reminiscences of Tolstoy* (trans. George Calderon), (New York: The Century Co., 1914), 323.

2. Tolstoy, *Reminiscences of Tolstoy*, 323.

3. Tolstoy, *Reminiscences of Tolstoy*, 326, 328.

4. Richard J. Foster and Dallas Willard, "Marriage and Divorce,"
   Quaker Life Magazine, 1973, www.dwillard.org/articles/artview
   .asp?artID=98, emphasis in original.

Chapter 10: What Would It Mean?
1. Dietrich Bonhoeffer quoted in *Bonhoeffer: Pastor, Martyr, Prophet,
   Spy: A Righteous Gentile Vs. the Third Reich* by Eric Metaxas,
   (Nashville, TN: Thomas Nelson, 2010), 137.

Chapter 12: Loneliness, the Ache
1. Tim Keller, *Counterfeit Gods: The Empty Promises of Money, Sex, and
   Power, and the Only Hope That Matters* (New York: Dutton, 2009), 38.
2. Henri J. Nouwen, *The Wounded Healer: Ministry in Contemporary
   Society* (New York: Doubleday, 1972), 85.
3. Nouwen, *Wounded Healer,* 84–85.
4. Marilynne Robinson, *Housekeeping* (New York: Farrar, Straus and
   Giroux, 1980), 152.
5. A. W. Tozer, *The Pursuit of God* (Rockville, MD: Serenity Publishers,
   2009), 20.

Chapter 13: Solitude, the Posture
1. Khalil Gibran, *The Prophet* (New York: Alfred A. Knopf, 1923), 17.
2. Dietrich Bonhoeffer, *Life Together* (New York: HarperOne, 1954),
   77–78.
3. Blaise Pascal, *Pensées* in *Foundations of the Christian Religion,*
   (Orlando, FL: Relevant Books, 2006), 42.
4. Henri J. M. Nouwen, *Seeds of Hope: A Nouwen Reader* (New York:
   Doubleday, 1989), 63.
5. Dallas Willard, foreword to *Invitation to Solitude and Silence:
   Experiencing God's Transforming Presence* by Ruth Haley Barton
   (Downers Grove, IL: InterVarsity Press, 2010), 12–13.

6. Thomas Merton, *Contemplative Prayer* (New York: Image, 1971), 10.
7. Thomas Merton, quoted in *Encounters with Merton* by Henri J. Nouwen (New York: The Crossroad Publishing Company, 1972), 67.

A Conclusion
1. Dietrich Bonhoeffer, *The Cost of Discipleship* (New York: Macmillan, 1959).

Appendix A: Questions and Answers
1. Rodney Clapp, *Families at the Crossroads: Beyond Traditional & Modern Options* (Downers Grove, IL: InterVarsity Press, 1993), 101, emphasis in original.
2. Marilynne Robinson, *The Death of Adam* (New York: Picador, 1998), 89.